100 THINGS
OILERS FANS
SHOULD KNOW & DO
BEFORE THEY DIE

100 THINGS OILERS FANS SHOULD KNOW & DO BEFORE THEY DIE

Joanne Ireland

TRIUMPH
BOOKS

No part of this publication may be reproduced, stored in a retrieval system, or transmitted in any form by any means, electronic, mechanical, photocopying, or otherwise, without the prior written permission of the publisher, Triumph Books LLC, 814 North Franklin Street, Chicago, Illinois 60610.

Library of Congress Cataloging-in-Publication Data is available upon request.

This book is available in quantity at special discounts for your group or organization. For further information, contact:

Triumph Books LLC
814 North Franklin Street
Chicago, Illinois 60610
(312) 337-0747
www.triumphbooks.com

Printed in U.S.A.
ISBN: 978-1-62937-373-7
Design by Patricia Frey
All photos courtesy of AP Images

For Blair and Scott, for hundreds of things

Contents

Foreword

I had made it through all the pre-draft interviews, but I had no idea what was to come. All I knew was that Tampa Bay's chief scout Tony Esposito had said to me that if I was still available at No. 8, I was going to the Lightning. Maybe that's why it was such a blur when I heard my name that day in Hartford—sixth overall—as a pick of the Edmonton Oilers.

I'd gone to Glen Sather's hockey school in Banff. I'd grown up watching and idolizing the Oilers, mimicking everything Wayne Gretzky did, right down to the jersey tuck—and now I was an Oiler. Most people don't get to live out their dreams in a lifetime, and here I was starting mine at 18.

I slept in my jersey that night—when I finally got to sleep. All the things I'd always dreamed of doing on the ice in an Oilers uniform played through my head. What I couldn't have imagined in those surreal moments was what a ride it would be: from my first game, lining up against my idol, to the last game trying to get that one last power play goal to beat Glenn Anderson's record. Never in all my highlight-reel imaginings did I ever think I'd get 19 years to do what I love at that level. There were gold medal wins with Team Canada, a memorable Stanley Cup run in 2006, and a trade that would forever change my life.

That trade.... We were still negotiating my contract with the Oilers in 2007, and I had told my agent, Donnie Meehan, I didn't want to worry about the contract stuff. I just wanted to play. I had seen lots of good teammates traded, and I guess I had never thought it would happen to me. Plus every negotiation I'd ever been through with the Oilers had been tough, so when they were going back and forth with my agent and nothing was happening, I went upstairs to rest, frustrated that I'd have to field questions about my contract instead of focusing on the game and Mark Messier's jersey retirement, which was also happening that night.

Next thing I knew, my mother-in-law was yelling up to my wife, Stacey, that there were reports I had been traded to New York. Earlier in the day they had reported that my contract was done, so I assumed they had it wrong again, but I picked up my phone and called Donnie. When he said yes, I was going to the Islanders, I just lost it. Stacey didn't know what to do with me. It's still kind of a blur. What I do remember is being stunned that I was watching Mark Messier Night from home…as an Islander.

My time in New York was short and emotional, but my Islanders teammates made it great. Mike Sillinger was awesome— he made everybody feel welcome, and we are good friends to this day. We made the playoffs that year for the first time in a long time. In exciting fashion too, winning the last game of the regular season in a shootout.

As great as the team was to my family and me, I was still in such a state after being traded from the Oilers that by the time I calmed down and started to think long term, it was almost July 1. This would be my first time as a free agent—something I had never even thought about. In the end, it was between Calgary and Colorado, but how do you head three hours south when you still really want to be an Oiler?

I just didn't feel it was right to go to the Flames, so when Colorado's Joe Sakic called and said they were going to try and make a run for it, it just made sense. Unfortunately, injuries plagued us, and when Joe retired in 2009 and Colorado decided they should go younger, it made sense to waive my no-trade clause.

The Kings seemed to be a good fit—maybe because they were good, fast, and young, or maybe because it was a big change from anything I'd known. Either way, we packed up again and moved to Hollywood.

Eventually, I just wanted to go back to Canada, to Edmonton. But the Oilers were going younger too, and weren't showing much interest. Winnipeg was really interested, and the Flames had a deal ready to go—a deal the Oilers must have gotten wind of, because suddenly they put in a call to Los Angeles...and the rest is history. I was an Oiler again, from 2011 until I retired in 2014.

The decision to retire really came down to choosing between my two options. I knew the Oilers weren't offering me another contract, so I either had to play my last NHL game with Edmonton or pick up my family and move them again. While my wife was supportive of whatever I chose to do, I really didn't know if I could see myself in a different uniform again. I really wanted to end my career as an Oiler.

The only other person I can think of who had an exit like mine was Wayne Gretzky, when he left New York. Being the greatest player to play the game, he deserved it. Did I deserve that? Probably not. But I was grateful for it, and very humbled.

I'm working with injured Oilers players now as a skills coach, again after some tough negotiations with Edmonton. I know what it's like to battle back from injury, so I can really relate to the players I'm helping.

It's nice to be back on the ice, and it allows me to remain a part of the team I've loved since I was a kid, only now I get to be at home with my family while I do it. I guess you could say I have the best of both worlds right now. Since Edmonton is our home, I take my kids to the rink for practices, or to games, and I have fun trying to be a fan.

I have to admit, though, there are times I wish I could still slip that jersey on and compete. It's been three years, and I still feel it! I'm guessing that part never goes away.

—Ryan Smyth

1 Memory Lane

On the corner of Wayne Gretzky Drive and 118th Avenue sits a concrete shell where only memories reside. Gone are the five Stanley Cup banners and the nine retired numbers that hung from the arena rafters. Gone too is the Gretzky statue that once stood outside the main doors, ushering in game-goers.

The vacated arena was home to the Edmonton Oilers for 42 years—right up until a bigger, better, brighter building opened in the city's downtown core. "Everyone feels like it's a fresh new start," Connor McDavid said after spending his first season in the NHL in Rexall Place. "It's tough to leave, it's sad and all that, but we have a shiny new building to go into, and everyone's excited about that."

The $17 million Edmonton Coliseum had opened on November 10, 1974, after a series of construction delays and labor strikes, and it was still a work in progress on opening night. The players had to dress and shower in the Edmonton Gardens—the Oilers' original home from 1972 until 1974—because their room wasn't finished, and seats were still being bolted into the stands when the game-goers started to arrive. Some guests were handed their cushions when they walked in.

Yes, there were kinks to work out, but the Coliseum was still a looker in its day, with its spacious interior and $120,000 game clock. "So beautifully functional, the comfortable sightlines from all seats, the wide walkways for meeting friends between periods, even radiating roof supports which glittered high overhead like the Aurora Borealis," local historian Tony Cashman wrote of the venue.

Tickets were $7 in 1974, at a time when the minimum wage in Alberta was $2.25 an hour. A season ticket for the Edmonton Eskimos of the Canadian Football League would have set you back $47.50. On opening night, in front of 15,326 spectators, the World Hockey Association's Oilers defeated the Cleveland Crusaders 4–1, scoring three third-period goals. Jacques Plante, captain Al Hamilton, Ken Brown, and Blair MacDonald were among the players in Edmonton's lineup.

A Piece of the Past

A battered blue metal door—a storied symbol of past playoff successes—is one of the club's iconic relics that was moved from the old arena. Plastered with decals and pockmarked with dents, it once stood outside the coaches' office, where it was within easy reach of a stick's butt end.

Mark Messier would let the coaches know the players were ready to go out for their warmup by butt-ending the door with his stick, a tradition that was later carried on by the overzealous Esa Tikkanen, who took it over the top, leaving sizeable indentations. "I don't think the first dent was on purpose, but many more followed," Messier said years later.

The Do It stickers that cover the door were holdovers from a fan giveaway early in the team's entry into the NHL. When the team won a playoff game, one of the decals was slapped onto the door, and soon a horizontal row appeared, representing each of the postseason wins. When the run ended with a championship, a silver facsimile of the Stanley Cup went up.

"It was a benchmark, a way for us to visually see where we stood as the playoffs went along. Every time we won a game, we put a sticker up on the door…it became more of a ritual," Messier said. "It became part of the folklore."

During a 2007 renovation, the door was moved into a hallway that led to the players' lounge, where its viewership was restricted. It now stands in the Hall of Fame room in the downtown arena for all to see.

Twenty nights later, Stevie Wonder played in the venue—the first of many concerts to be staged in a building that would become the bedrock for the arrival of the National Hockey League. The Edmonton Gardens was torn down in 1982—three years after the merger of the WHL and NHL.

"[The Coliseum is] an amazing place, a huge part of hockey history, and it probably housed some of the best teams and some of the best players that ever played the game," said Doug Weight, who spent nine years with the Oilers, two as the team captain. "It's a very special place."

The Edmonton Coliseum was renamed Northlands Coliseum in 1978, was later known as Skyreach Center, and in 2003 it was christened Rexall Place. Through the years, the scoreboard was upgraded, more suites were added, and in 2007 the locker room underwent a $3 million renovation. But the 16,839-seat venue was definitely showing its age by the time the Oilers played their last game there on April 6, 2016, defeating the Vancouver Canucks 6–2.

Gretzky was there for the final game, and so were Mark Messier, Paul Coffey, and Grant Fuhr. More than 100 players from the club's past gathered to say good-bye to a building that hosted 1,431 regular-season games, 129 playoff games, and four Stanley Cup celebrations.

The Coliseum also played host to the 1981 Canada Cup, the gymnastics competition of the 1978 Commonwealth Games, the 1996 World Figure Skating Championships, and the 1989 NHL All-Star Game, and it has been home to the Canadian Finals Rodeo for more than four decades. It was even at the heart of a fight between former owner Peter Pocklington and Northlands, which was serving as the arena's guardian, back when both sides were fighting for control of concert and concession revenues.

"Incredible memories," Mark Messier said when he returned for the farewell game. "Building the Northlands Coliseum in 1974 put us on the map."

2 The Early Years

Edmonton lacks the cachet that comes from sprouting one of the league's Original Six franchises, but there is an abundance of interesting historical links tying the city to the game.

1. The first recorded hockey game in Edmonton was on December 25, 1894, and pit the Thistles and Strathcona.
2. That shiny new downtown arena that opened in 2016? Not the first. That distinction belongs to the Thistle Rink, a 2,000-seat multiuse venue that was built by local businessman Dick Secord in 1902. When it burned down in 1912, it hastened the need for an ice sheet to be installed in the new pavilion being assembled on the fairgrounds of the Edmonton Exhibition Association, later known as Northlands.

   The new arena opened on Christmas Day 1913, with 2,000 fans on hand to watch the Dominion Furriers play the hometown Edmonton Eskimos hockey team. A bleacher seat could be had for 50 cents while a box seat was priced at a dollar. Playing goal for the Furriers was Court May, brother of Canadian flying ace Wop May.

   Following the Second World War, another 1,200 seats were added to the arena—at a cost of $163,000—and the name was changed to the Edmonton Gardens. Condemned by a fire marshal in 1966, some necessary renovations only bought the building more time. It continued to operate until the construction of the 16,000-seat Coliseum on the former site of the Hayward Lumber Company. The Coliseum was going to be the new home of the World Hockey Association's Oilers.
3. The first Stanley Cup challenge for Edmonton unfolded in 1908. Teams challenged for the championship back in the early

1900s, and Edmonton's Eskimos made a couple runs at the trophy, which was to be awarded to the top amateur team in the country until professional teams were allowed to compete for it beginning in 1906.

In their first Cup challenge of 1908, the Eskimos—with recruits such as the commanding Lester Patrick in their lineup—lost to the Montreal Wanderers in the two-game set. Edmonton challenged again in 1909–10 but couldn't overtake the Ottawa Senators.

By 1923 the Stanley Cup Finals were a three-team contest with the Oilers falling again to the Senators, who had 21-year-old Frank "King" Clancy in their lineup. Clancy played goal for two minutes in the second game of the series after Clint Benedict was sent off to serve a penalty. He didn't allow a goal, but more important, he proved to be so versatile that he played all six positions in the game. Fans who wanted to follow the action stood outside the *Edmonton Journal*'s downtown building, listening to the broadcast through loudspeakers that had been set up for the occasion.

4. The great Eddie Shore—better known then as the Edmonton Express—played for the Eskimos before he left for the NHL. He also wasn't the only one who cultivated his craft in Edmonton while playing for the city's senior and juniors teams. Pat Quinn, Glenn Hall, Norm Ullman, Johnny Bucyk, Glen Sather, Bud Poile, and Al Arbour were among those who eventually graduated to the big leagues.

5. Clarence Campbell—the man for whom the Western Conference trophy is named—also has ties to Edmonton. He attended Strathcona High School and obtained his law degree at the University of Alberta, then supplemented his income by refereeing. A Rhodes Scholar who represented Canada as a lawyer at the Nuremberg trials, Campbell went on to serve as president of the NHL from 1946 to 1977. He even had a

hand in building Renfrew Park, which was the first ballpark in Edmonton's river valley.

6. In the Oilers' first season of the WHA, Jacques Plante, who changed the face of modern goaltending, signed on for two seasons, though his agreement—which paid him $150,000 a season—stipulated he would only play home games. He was 46 years old at the time, and played in the first WHA game at the Coliseum on November 10, 1974, against the Cleveland Crusaders and their goaltender Gerry Cheevers. He didn't return for a second season.

7. The Edmonton Flyers were the toast of their hometown after winning the Allan Cup in 1948. Canada's senior men's hockey champions defeated the Ottawa Senators four games to one. They were showered with gifts, collected the key to the city, and were feted in a parade down Jasper Avenue. "The biggest concentration of enthusiastic humanity of its kind in the city's history—estimated at 60,000—jammed Jasper Avenue, street intersections and Market Square to hail the Flyers," was the dispatch printed in the *Edmonton Journal*.

   Pug Young was named honorary police chief for two weeks. The captain of the team was Gordie Watt, who became a father that week. He named his son Allan. He would become the Oilers' vice president of marketing and communications, a post he held until 2012, when he left for the Edmonton Eskimos football club.

8. And then there were the Edmonton Waterloo Mercurys, who not only represented Canada at the 1952 Winter Olympics in Oslo, Norway, but also claimed the gold medal. It turned out to be an even more notable achievement given it wasn't until 2002 that the country captured another Olympic title.

3 Wild Bill

Few had what it took to go toe-to-toe with Bill Hunter in any sort of hyperbole set-to, but for all his bluster, few promoted the game like Hunter did. This was a man who once called a press conference to announce he was going to have a press conference the following day. A tireless promoter, general manager, and coach, Hunter was also one of the Oilers' founding fathers. He was Edmonton's link to the NHL.

Better known as Wild Bill—a name he inherited from a referee after a heated dispute, but one he claimed he wasn't all that fond of—there was no dismissing Hunter's fiery nature. He often fired his coaches, even dismissing Bill Gadsby during a playoff run. One of his favorite retorts if anyone questioned him was: "If you don't believe me, you're a goddamned liar." And he once told his players, who were waiting to board a plane: "We'll board last, men, so we get our choice of seats."

"In the hockey circle, especially in Edmonton, [Wild Bill] should be immortalized," Kevin Lowe, the Oilers' tie to the past and present, once said. "The greatness of Gretzky and Messier and the championship teams…maybe one of the greatest teams of all time…is linked to him, because if it wasn't for his efforts, the team wouldn't have been there. And it's more than that. It's just the legend, and all the things he did. I said to someone my goal is to win the Stanley Cup, but it would be nice to orchestrate the media the way he did."

Instrumental in the formation of the World Hockey Association in 1972, as well as Edmonton's entry into the new league, Hunter campaigned for a new arena for his Oilers, and never dismissed the dream of his team one day playing in the NHL. The Coliseum, the rink Hunter pushed so hard for, opened on November 10, 1974. He was there, of course. And he was there the night the Oilers played their first NHL game—as a guest of owner Peter Pocklington.

"It was Bill who is the reason it all happened, and you forget about that. The Oilers are here, and that's that. But somebody went to an awful lot of aggravation to make it happen. Hockey fans and Oiler fans and the community owe Bill Hunter such a debt of gratitude," said Cal Nichols, who chaired the ownership group after Pocklington's era.

Edmonton hadn't had a pro team since the Edmonton Flyers were shuttered by their parent team, the Detroit Red Wings, in 1963, so when Hunter brought the Alberta Oilers to Edmonton in 1972, it ended a long absence. Their first game, in Ottawa against the Nationals, was televised on CBC—one of six WHA games to be broadcast that season. The Oilers won 7–4.

The mission of the World Hockey Association was to compete against the National Hockey League by bringing professional hockey to new markets, and it took root after the Winnipeg Jets lured star Bobby Hull away from the Chicago Blackhawks with a $1 million signing bonus. All the WHA teams anted up to pay a portion of the contract to ensure credibility, and ticket sales. There was also the draw of watching Gordie Howe playing on the Houston Aeros with his sons Mark and Marty, but even the star power failed to trump the league's money issues.

There were unpaid bills, franchises that folded or relocated, and lawsuits, and even though the Oilers were one of the more stable franchises, eventually Hunter's tenure ran its course as well. Shortly after he was directed by his business partners to step down as GM, the team was sold to Nelson Skalbania, who then flipped the team to Pocklington.

In 1979 the Oilers, Quebec Nordiques, Jets, and New England Whalers gained entry into the NHL, and the WHA folded after the

Jets defeated the Oilers for the Avco Cup. Dave Semenko scored Edmonton's last WHA goal.

Hunter, meanwhile, didn't slow down. After spending a year as the advertising sales director of the *Edmonton Sun*, Hunter, the man who helped orchestrate the 1974 series pitting the WHA All-Stars against the Soviets, moved on. He was behind a bid to bring the NHL's St. Louis Blues to his hometown of Saskatoon, recruiting backers to build the town's 18,000-seat arena, which stands as a testament to how close he came to seeing that plan through. The NHL eventually refused to transfer the Blues to such a small market. But Hunter's reach was that long.

"He meant a lot to Edmonton and to our family. He's an inspiration to all of us," local product Mike Comrie said in 2002, adding that one of the reasons he signed in Edmonton was because of Hunter. "It's unbelievable the life he lived…he [is] the main reason the NHL is in Edmonton. He was an unbelievable man."

He led an incredible life indeed. After flying with the Royal Canadian Air Force in World War II, Hunter dabbled in the broadcasting business before opening a sporting goods store in his home province. By the age of 23, he was the owner, manager, and coach of the Regina Capitals hockey team. What followed was a tireless undertaking as a coach, general manager, and owner of numerous teams and organizations.

In the mid-1960s he accepted an offer to run the junior Oil Kings and was soon behind the formation of the Western Hockey League, in spite of resistance from the NHL. He even took over ownership of the club from the Detroit Red Wings, setting up an office in Edmonton's Hotel Macdonald. One of his first orders of business was to move the team from the Jasper Place Arena (now the Bill Hunter Arena) to the Edmonton Gardens so he could sell more tickets.

The Oil Kings won two championships in Wild Bill's first go-round, but the club was not nearly as successful the second time around. Hunter had rustled up a partnership deal with Vic Mah and Wayne Tennant to bring back the Oil Kings after his time had expired in the WHA. The group couldn't make a go of it, and the team was sold.

But when he later joined forces with ownership partners Dr. Charles Allard and Zane Feldman to bring the Alberta Oilers to Edmonton, he sold the city on his dream, taking out billboards that shouted: WORLD HOCKEY COMES TO TOWN and FOLLOW THE CROWD. BUY NOW.

He managed to sign goaltender Jacques Plante to a two-year contract, and when he inked center Jim Harrison to a four-year contract with a bonus of $75,000, he arranged for a photo op in which the center was pushing a shopping cart full of cash. That was Hunter.

He was inducted into the Canadian Sports Hall of Fame in 2001 and was also honored by the Order of Canada. "He's just Father Hockey in Edmonton," said Rod Phillips, the former radio voice of the Oilers. "There was no battle he didn't think he could win." But of course there was one he couldn't win; Hunter lost his battle with bone cancer on December 16, 2002, at the age of 82.

In keeping with his Mr. Hockey persona, he even wanted souvenir pucks handed out at his funeral, which drew a host of dignitaries, sports figures, and television cameras. "He would love this. This is a sellout," said former Oil King and Oiler Al Hamilton, one of four eulogists. "I think he flirted with the idea of charging for this but he thought that might be a little tacky. Instead, my friend Bill decided there would be an exit fee of $50."

4 Humble Beginnings

When brash owner Peter Pocklington proclaimed in 1979 that within five years, Edmonton would have the Stanley Cup, few paid him much heed. And rightly so, or so it seemed. The beginning was a humble one. The Oilers lost their first game as an NHL franchise—a 4–2 decision to the Blackhawks in Chicago on October 10, 1979—and finished their opening season with a record of 28–39–13. The Oilers used six goaltenders that season and surrendered 322 goals while scoring 301. Dave Dryden, Eddie Mio, Jim Corsi, Ron Low, Don Cutts, and Bob Dupuis all saw time in Edmonton's net in 1979–1980.

Through their first 20 games, they were a mere 3–12–5, and on the heels of one of their early three-game losing streaks, Mark Messier was sent to the team's minor league affiliate in Houston for four games. He was late for a team flight a day earlier, which turned out to be the tipping point for Coach Glen Sather.

When March 1980 dawned, things didn't look particularly promising either, with the team on a dismal stretch that saw them go 1–10–0. Something had to change. "We got together one day

Remember When?

Even Wayne Gretzky was overcome with a touch of stage fright on opening night in Chicago Stadium, particularly in the game's early going when he took his first draw against Stan Mikita—his dad's favorite player. Gretzky did not win the faceoff.

"I was too nervous," Gretzky said recently when he was recalling some of his favorite NHL memories. "I kept looking at him...I think they had dropped the puck and I didn't even know it had been dropped."

Shown here in 1978 with the Indianapolis Racers, Wayne Gretzky proved to be the best thing that ever happened to the Edmonton Oilers.

and said, 'We have to start working.' When we did, everything came into place," Stan Weir said after the team closed its inaugural campaign with eight wins and two losses, securing the last of the 16 playoff spots in the 21-team league.

In their final regular-season game, they beat Don Cherry's Colorado Rockies 6–2 then squared off against the top-ranked Philadelphia Flyers in the opening round of the playoffs. The Flyers took it in three straight games, although the Oilers did take them to double overtime in Game 3. "They should be damn proud of themselves in that dressing room," said Flyers coach Pat Quinn. "They showed us their mettle. They showed us what they're made of and what they're going to do in the future."

Wayne Gretzky, in spite of trying to stave off a bout of tonsillitis in his rookie NHL season, finished with 51 goals and 137 points, nearly equaling the work of the Los Angeles Kings' Marcel

The Oilers' Opening Day Lineup on October 10, 1979, in Chicago

Goal: Dave Dryden, Eddie Mio

Defense: Kevin Lowe, Lee Fogolin, Doug Hicks, Colin Campbell, Pat Price, Risto Siltanen

Forwards: Wayne Gretzky, Blair MacDonald, Brett Callighen, Mark Messier, Stan Weir, Dave Lumley, Dave Hunter, Ron Chipperfield (C), Dave Semenko, Peter Driscoll, Bill Flett

And on the other side?

Goal: Tony Esposito, Mike Veisor

Defense: Dave Logan, Keith Magnuson (C), Bob Murray, Mike O'Connell, Greg Fox, Doug Wilson

Forwards: Doug Lecuyer, Terry Ruskowski, Reg Kerr, John Marks, Tom Lysiak, Tim Higgins, Rich Preston, Cliff Koroll, Grant Mulvey, J.P. Bordeleau, Stan Mikita

Dionne. Dionne finished with 53 goals and 137 points to take the scoring title. It marked only the second time two players finished with the same point total. (Bobby Hull and Andy Bathgate had finished with 84 points in 1961–62; Hull won it with 50 goals, compared to the 28 Bathgate netted.) "It's a little discouraging to tie for a scoring title…and still lose," Gretzky said. "I'm going to have to shape up next season. My dad told me to never be happy with finishing second."

Gretzky missed out on the rookie trophy as well, after the league decreed he was not eligible because he had played in the WHA.

5 Edmonton, Meet Stanley

Thirty years after introducing Edmonton to the Stanley Cup, yesterday's heroes reconvened for a long-overdue after-party. The waistlines had expanded, the hair had grayed, but the memories were still fresh when the 1984 team reassembled for the Legacy Reunion. Funds raised from the reunion went to the Edmonton Oilers Ambulatory Clinic at the Stollery Children's Hospital.

Jari Kurri flew in from Finland, Jaroslav Pouzar from the Czech Republic, and Rick Chartraw made the trek from his home in Australia. Chartraw played just one playoff game in 1984, so he didn't get his name engraved on the Stanley Cup, but he was still a part of the team, a part of the celebration. It was the first time the team had been together since winning the championship. Peter Pocklington was there too, and this time the former owner who was once castigated for trading Wayne Gretzky received a standing ovation. Time does heal all wounds.

"This team had such pizzazz and flair about it, so many Hall of Famers...it was the perfect formula for memories," said Dave Lumley, who will long be remembered for scoring the empty-net goal that put the finishing touch on the 5–2 win over the New York Islanders on May 19, 1984.

Just five years after joining the NHL, the Oilers had captured the Stanley Cup. Only the 1940 New York Rangers were younger when they accomplished the feat, winning it in their third season. It was the first of five Stanley Cup championships the Oilers would win, their first of four on home ice, and it marked the end of the Islanders' reign. "I felt no shame turning the puck over to them," Islanders captain Denis Potvin said the night their quest for a fifth straight Stanley Cup came to an end. "One great team turning it over to a team that was great all year."

The Oilers had already made their mark on the league with their dynamic offensive skills and their trip to the championship finals just one year earlier. The 1983–84 team then proceeded to win 57 games while scoring a remarkable 446 goals to finish first overall. They knocked off the Winnipeg Jets 3–0 in the postseason, eliminated the Calgary Flames in a seven-game set, then rolled over the Minnesota North Stars 4–0, setting up another showdown with the Islanders.

But the Islanders had not only crushed the Oilers' playoff hopes the year before, they were on a quest to secure their place in history as a dynasty. It was not going to be an easy test. Edmonton goaltender Grant Fuhr outdueled future Hall of Famer Billy Smith in a 1–0 victory in the opening game, then the Islanders responded with a commanding 6–1 victory in Game 2. When the series moved to Edmonton, the Oilers posted back-to-back 7–2 wins.

Prime Minister Brian Mulroney was in the building for Game 5, sitting with Pocklington amongst the frenzied hometown fans. The Oilers had built a 4–0 lead, but 35 seconds into the third, the Islanders got a pair of goals from rookie Pat LaFontaine, who set an NHL record for the quickest two goals to start a period.

That would be it for the Islanders. Soon the Coliseum was awash in blue and orange balloons; sparklers lit up the stands. It was the sparklers that videographer Don Metz remembered. He was filming the game from the concourse level, and just as Lumley shot the puck into an empty net, he happened to look over to a nearby section. One of the fan's jackets was on fire. "He didn't care. The people in front of him didn't care," Metz said during an interview with 630 CHED. "Eventually they put it out, but it was just another of those moments."

It was a moment that was replayed 30 years later at the Legacy Reunion, in a city that has never tired of reliving the championship and the team that went on to win again in 1985, 1987, 1988, and once without their leading man—Wayne Gretzky—in 1990.

"Where else would you ever get 17,000 people to come back just to listen to us talk about what we used to do in 1984?" Gretzky mused during the Legacy Reunion. "We were kids, and we thought we knew everything. We didn't, but we knew how to play hockey."

"It kind of reminds me of Grade 10, back in high school, when everybody goes their separate ways in the summer," Lumley said. "Now take away how everybody looks…and it's like it was only three months ago that we were all together."

Gretzky had a heavy hand in getting the players together. They needed no encouragement to be transported back 30 years. "To this day, you get shivers when you think about it," Mark Messier said in a documentary following the Oilers. "Being on the ice, and watching the clock count down and realizing you're a Stanley Cup champion…pretty incredible moment."

"The first thing I remember is after the second period of the final game," Gretzky added. "We were winning 4–0 and Glen Sather [was] saying, 'You have one more good period and you guys are going to remember this for life. This is a moment in time you guys will never forget.' And here we are 30 years later, and it's exactly what he said.

Mark Messier smiles after being awarded the Conn Smythe Trophy.

"It feels like it was yesterday. We're all a little bigger, we're all a bit slower, we're all obviously older, but the memory of winning that Cup seems like it was yesterday—and that will never go away."

6 Magic Moments

Ask anyone who had the good fortune of following the human highlight reel that was Wayne Gretzky, and more often than not, the moment that stands out is the night he revised the NHL record book, scoring his 50th goal in his 39th game.

Rod Phillips had settled into his customary spot in the broadcast booth up in the catwalk of the Coliseum on December 30, 1981, to run through his usual pregame routine in advance of the game against the Philadelphia Flyers. What the play-by-play ace didn't do was prepare a magnificent call that he could pull out in the event that Gretzky was able to make history. What was the point? The 20-year-old center was still five goals shy of passing the record of 50 goals in 50 games first established by Montreal Canadiens legend Maurice "Rocket" Richard in 1944 then equaled by Mike Bossy of the New York Islanders 36 years later.

The Oilers star was going to do it, it was just a matter of when. Even Gretzky figured it would take another game or two. He had planned to have his parents fly to Vancouver, where the Oilers were playing next, because that's when he figured the countdown would really heat up. But that night against the Flyers, he scored two first-period goals, one in the second, and another in the third, then with just three seconds left on the clock, he scored into an empty net.

The players cleared the bench to congratulate their teammate, and 17,490 fans were on their feet saluting their star with an ovation that lasted long past the game's end. The ice was littered with programs, and up in the booth, Phillips was calling the historic goal. "It was basically a breakaway on an empty net, and Gretz got the puck at center ice," said Phillips. "I just remember saying, 'Will he shoot? He does. He scooooooooooores!'

"It was kind of a stupid call, because naturally he was going to shoot. But somewhere in the back of my mind I was thinking, *Well, maybe he doesn't want his 50th goal into an empty net.* So I say, 'Will he shoot?' Of course he's going to shoot. Everybody in the rink knew he was going to. It wasn't the greatest call of all time."

Phillips had plenty of opportunities to make more memorable calls. Gretzky had his name attached to 61 NHL records when he retired from the game—a few that were shared and some that may never be broken—and many of them were set while he was with the Oilers.

But it was the night he shattered the 50 in 50 standard that trumps his long list of magic moments. Even by his own lofty standards. "People ask me all the time about my records, but to me, that's my favorite," he said in an interview with Canada.com. "They're all made to be broken, that's what sports is. That's what's so great about sports, but that's my favorite because I think that will be the hardest to break."

Gretzky went on to score 92 goals that 80-game season, demolishing the 11-year-old record of 76 held by Phil Esposito—again, another record that will surely stand the test of time. Of the 417 goals the team racked up that season, the playmaker extraordinaire was involved in more than half of them (92 goals, 120 assists).

"What he did was absolutely amazing," said Pete Peeters, who was in net for the Flyers that night. "I wouldn't have done anything differently on his other goals."

"Any superlatives I might offer would be inadequate," added Flyers coach Pat Quinn.

Gretzky had scored in eight straight games before setting the record—racking up 14 in total, including four against the Los Angeles Kings in a 10–3 rout one game earlier.

"He had told his [mom and dad] that they probably should fly to Vancouver," Kevin Lowe told NHL.com when he was asked about his memories of that night. "Then he phoned his dad after the game from a pay phone in the hallway to tell him not to bother coming."

A Few of the Great One's Greatest Moments

Record-Setting Numbers

Most regular-season goals, career: 894 (in 1,485 games)
Playoff goals, career: 122
Most goals in a season: 92 (1981–82)
Most goals in one season, including playoffs: 100 (1983–84: 87 goals in 74 regular-season games, 13 goals in 19 playoff games)
Most points in a single season: 215 (1985–86)
Games scoring three or more goals, career: 50
Game-winning goals in the playoffs, career: 24
Playoff games scoring three or more goals: 10
Seasons scoring 50+ goals: 9
Seasons scoring 60+ goals: 5 (four of which were consecutive)
Seasons scoring 100+ points: 15 (13 were sequential)
Points, including playoffs: 3,239
Highest points-per-game average, season: 2.77 (1983–84)
Most goals in the first 50 games of a season: 61 (1981–82, and again in 1983–84)
Consecutive point-scoring streak: 51 games (1983–84)
Fastest to 50 goals from start of season: 39 games (1981–82)

Single-Game Records

Assists (tied): 7 (three times)
  • February 15, 1980, vs. Washington
  • December 11, 1985, vs. Chicago
  • February 14, 1986, vs. Quebec
Goals, one period (tied): 4 vs. St. Louis on February 18, 1981

Playoff Records, One Year
Points: 47 in 1985
Assists: 31 in 1988

Playoff Records in One Series
Points, Finals: 13 in 1988 vs. Boston
Assists, Finals: 10 in 1988 vs. Boston

Youngest to Score 50 goals in One Season
Accomplished in 1981–82, at 19 years, 2 months, and 7 days old

Milestones
Most goals, one game: 5 (four times)
 • February 18, 1981, vs. St. Louis
 • December 30, 1981, vs. Philadelphia
 • December 15, 1984, vs. St. Louis
 • December 6, 1987, vs. Minnesota

Most penalty minutes, one game: 20
 • November 4, 1989, vs. Hartford (two misconducts)

Fighting majors: 3
 • With Doug Lecuyer (Chicago), March 14, 1980
 • With Neal Broten (Minnesota), December 22, 1982
 • With Bob Murray (Chicago), March 7, 1984
First point: October 10, 1979, vs. Chicago (assist)
First goal: October 14, 1979, vs. Vancouver (Glen Hanlon)
100th goal: March 7, 1981, vs. Philadelphia (empty net)
500th goal: November 22, 1986, vs. Vancouver (empty net)
1,000th assist: November 4, 1987, vs. Rangers
802nd goal: March 23, 1994, vs. Vancouver (Kirk McLean)
1,050th assist: March 1, 1988, vs. Los Angeles
1,851st point: October 15, 1989, vs. Edmonton (goal)
2,000th NHL point: October 26, 1990, vs. Winnipeg
2,500th NHL point: April 17, 1995, vs. Calgary
Last goal: March 29, 1999, vs. Islanders (Wade Flaherty)
Last point: April 18, 1999, vs. Pittsburgh (assist)

NHL Trophies
Hart Trophy (most valuable player): 1980, 1981, 1982, 1983, 1984,
 1985, 1986, 1987, and 1989

NHL Trophies (continued)
Art Ross Trophy (scoring championship): 1981, 1982, 1983, 1984,
    1985, 1986, 1987, 1990, 1991, and 1994
Lady Byng Trophy (most gentlemanly player): 1980, 1991, 1992,
    1994, and 1999
Conn Smythe Trophy (playoff MVP): 1985 and 1988
Lester B. Pearson Award (league MVP as selected by the players):
    1982, 1983, 1984, 1985, and 1987
Lester Patrick Trophy (contribution to hockey in the US): 1994

Miscellanea
The most games Gretzky played consecutively without registering a
point was four, and it was during his time with the New York Rangers.
He had two three-game pointless streaks with the Oilers and four
three-game stretches with the Los Angeles Kings.
    Gretzky's longest point-scoring streak was 51 games (with
Edmonton), doubling his next-longest, which was a 25-game streak
he put together with the Kings.

7 The Architect

For more than two decades, Glen "Slats" Sather was synonymous
with the Oilers. He was with the team in its early journey through
the World Hockey Association, and he was integral to its success in
the National Hockey League. He was a coach and general manager,
a mentor. He was the dean of a dynasty.

"Slats was the straw that stirred the drink that got us all together
and on the same path, and that's what's so special about him," said
Glenn Anderson, one of his many disciples. "Glen Sather was kind
of the staple that put us all together and did everything that we
needed to do to be successful."

"The first thing I think about when I think of Glen is his competitiveness," said Mark Messier, another of Sather's draft picks, who was inducted into the Hockey Hall of Fame in 2007. "He absolutely would not accept losing. And even when we lost, he would not accept quitting. He always believed we had another opportunity to do better."

Having Wayne Gretzky to build a team around was certainly a significant advantage, but Sather surrounded him with a brilliant group of draft picks—and then he managed all their egos and kept the group committed even after they had tasted success. He molded the game to suit their speed and skill, leading an expansion team to the Stanley Cup in just five years. His Oilers would go on to win another four championships—all within the short span of seven years.

"None of this would have happened without Glen Sather," said Kevin Lowe, the first player drafted, now the vice president of the Oilers Entertainment Group. "He really instilled a belief in us.... I think back to the early days playing the likes the Montreal Canadiens, the Philadelphia Flyers, the Boston Bruins, New York Islanders, and he really emphasized that we could be every bit as good. He had a great deal of swagger and confidence, and when he said you will be, we believed him."

Sather was the architect of a team that won four Stanley Cups while he was head coach and general manager, and a fifth with him as team president. He was able to keep the team together for as long as he did because there were no salary disclosures, and when he had holes, he found a way to fill them. The Oilers won their fifth Cup with only seven players left from the team that won the first.

He cajoled, he criticized, he did whatever he thought it would take. There were team outings on snowmobiles, hunting trips, and even a tutorial on tying ties in the team's early years. "I wanted them experiencing things other than playing hockey and being a celebrity. They needed other activities in life to give them some purpose other than hanging around a bar. So we'd introduce them to fishing or target shooting. Or Ski-Dooing, which looking back was a little risky. We had some good times," said Sather, an Albertan who played for the Edmonton Oil Kings' Memorial Cup team in 1963 before playing for Boston, Pittsburgh, the New York Rangers, St. Louis, Montreal, and Minnesota over his nine seasons in the NHL.

Sather liked reclamation projects, and he liked autonomy. He grew tired of having to answer to the 38 owners in the Edmonton Investors Group and cut his ties with the team after the 1999–2000 season, moving on to the New York Rangers. "Essentially, this marks the end of an era," said Messier of Sather's departure. And it was. Some of Sather's tactics wouldn't work in today's world, but they certainly did then.

Inducted into the Hockey Hall of Fame in 1997 as a builder, his banner went up into the rafters in Edmonton in 2015. It was the ninth time an Oiler was honored, a rare distinction for an executive in the NHL. Fittingly, his was the last banner to go up before the team moved to their new arena.

"I remember vividly when Don Cherry made disparaging remarks about Randy Gregg's ability [on *Hockey Night in Canada*]," Lowe said. "Glen made Don come and apologize at a team lunch."

Another time, Messier and Lowe showed up late for a practice during a road trip in Los Angeles, and Sather was not impressed. "He told me and Mark, 'I want you to climb the stairs at the L.A. Forum with your skates and equipment on. Since you weren't interested in practice today, you can sit up there and watch,'" Lowe recalled. "After we did that for about five minutes, he called us down and put the whole team in the stands, and he left Mark and [me] out on the ice to skate."

The Night(s) the Lights Went Out

With the temperature in the aging Boston Garden hovering around 28 degrees Celsius—and no air-conditioning to negate the humidity in the 60-year-old arena—fog was soon rolling out over the ice during the 1988 Stanley Cup Finals between the Bruins and Oilers on May 24. The fog turned out to be just one of the oddities that unfolded on a night that has earned its place amongst the NHL's more unconventional playoff moments. That same night, the lights went out, leading to the cancellation of the game. IT'S AN OUT(R)AGE! trumpeted a headline in the *Boston Herald* the morning after.

The game had already been frequently delayed by referee Denis Morel, who instructed the players to move around the ice to disperse the thick, heavy fog. "You could feel it on your face," Mike Krushelnyski told the *Edmonton Journal*'s Cam Cole. "If you were skating down low, bent over, it was like a sauna…but if you straightened up, so your head was above it, it was like, 'Ahhhh, fresh air.' You couldn't see 10 feet in front of you in some places."

Five times the game was delayed because of the fog. Then just after Edmonton's Craig Simpson had tipped a Steve Smith point shot past Andy Moog to tie the game 3–3 with 3:23 to go in the second, the lights went out. A 4,000-volt switch overloaded on a transformer outside the building, tripping the switch and shutting down the building's main power source.

The power was restored, but by then most of the fans had been evacuated, and NHL president John Ziegler had reached a decision after meeting with the team owners and general managers. Calling the outage an act of God and citing bylaw 27-12, which stipulates in such an emergency the game must be replayed in its entirety, if necessary, at the end of the series. He went on to announce that the fourth game of the championship Finals had been canceled and that teams would just move on to Edmonton. The Celtics had the building booked for an NBA game the following night.

"I'm not saying we're happy with it," said Boston general manager Harry Sinden, "but we're a member of this league and we must live with it. The bylaw really told us what we had to do. It seems to me it was probably put in by some of the old-timers in the league to prevent someone from pulling a switch."

Another Year, Another Outage

One taxing overtime period gave way to the next, only to be followed by another on opening night of the 1990 Stanley Cup Finals between the Oilers and the Bruins. It was hot in the Boston Garden, and it was humid. It was an endurance test for the two deadlocked teams. And again, darkness descended.

In the third overtime period, with the teams knotted at 2–2, a circuit breaker controlling the television lights blew. It was, at least, a relatively quick fix. After a 30-minute delay, the power was restored and the players returned to the ice to continue the marathon that finally ended when Petr Klima, who had spent long stretches of the game on the bench, beat Andy Moog at 1:22 AM Eastern to give the Oilers a 3–2 victory.

"When I first got out there, I wanted to be careful more than anything else; three and a half hours is a long time between shifts," said Klima. "And then when I got the puck, I figured it was 1:30 in the morning and so I'd better make a good shot." It took 115 minutes and 13 seconds to play a game that started on May 15 and ended a day later, gaining status as the longest game ever played in the Stanley Cup Finals.

Edmonton goaltender Bill Ranford made 50 saves, the Bruins' Craig Janney was whisked off in an ambulance with dehydration after the second period, and as the night wore on, the Zamboni even had to be refueled. "I got more ice time in that game than I did in my third year in the NHL," said Cam Neely, Boston's star winger.

"Thank God it was only one loss," Moog said. "If they had counted it as two because of the number of periods, we'd be in real trouble."

As it turned out, the power failure just delayed the inevitable. Two days later, in Edmonton, the Oilers scored a 6–3 victory to sweep the best-of-seven series and extend their playoff record to 16–2. For a franchise that was just nine years old, the Oilers had wasted no time making their mark. They had not only made five Cup appearances in six years, they had won four of the last five championships. The word *dynasty* had seeped into conversations about the team. "A great, great team beat us," said Boston coach Terry O'Reilly.

"As a coach, when you lose to them, you say they're great—you have to," Detroit coach Jacques Demers told the *Journal*. "But now I'm sitting here as a fan, close to the ice surface, watching it from above, and…it's brilliant. They're so deliberate, so methodical."

The Day That Changed the Game

Of all the images woven through Edmonton's historical repository, it is the image of a teary-eyed Wayne Gretzky sitting behind an expanse of microphones that best depicts the day that changed the game—in Edmonton and in the NHL. He cried, a city wept, and the country gasped when it was announced that Canada's hockey icon had been traded to the Los Angeles Kings. But that staggering August 9, 1988, trade turned out to be the stimulus for the league's expansion into the Sun Belt states.

"If you're a kid, you like stars, and Wayne Gretzky was the biggest of all time. He was hockey's Michael Jordan," Dave Ogrean—the executive director of USA Hockey—told the *Edmonton Journal*'s John MacKinnon 25 years after the trade. "He was the Pied Piper for our sport in the US. After he moved to L.A., hockey became something to pursue as opposed to something to do."

Gretzky, Marty McSorley, and Mike Krushelnyski went to Los Angeles in exchange for Jimmy Carson, Martin Gelinas, three first-round draft picks, and $15 million US. That last component was the pivotal piece for Oilers owner Peter Pocklington, who was under pressure from the Alberta Treasury Branch to make a payment on his line of credit.

"The Edmonton Oilers without Wayne Gretzky is like apple pie without ice cream, like winter without snow, like...*Wheel of Fortune* without Vanna White...it's quite simply unthinkable," New Democratic Party Member of Parliament Nelson Riis said at the time, urging the federal government to stop the sale. There was just too much money on the table. Pocklington was not going to reject the deal. Not given his certainty that Gretzky was a depreciating asset in the twilight years of his contract.

Kings owner Bruce McNall, meanwhile, was intent on making hockey relevant in Los Angeles and had continually been asking Pocklington what it would take to acquire Gretzky. He finally got his answer, and not all that long after the Oilers won their fourth Stanley Cup—and only a month after the fairy-tale wedding of Gretzky and actress Janet Jones—Pocklington pulled the trigger on one of the biggest trades in pro sports. McNall, who had assumed control of the Kings that year, had his cornerstone; Canadian fans had nothing but outrage.

"Wayne Gretzky is a national symbol, like the beaver," Riis continued in his plea from Parliament Hill. "How can we allow the sale of our national symbols?"

"It's like ripping the heart out of a city," Edmonton mayor Laurence Decore said that day.

The trade also injected an element of big business into the game or, at the very least, drove home the point that times were

In the Thicke of It

The late Alan Thicke, best known for his role as Dr. Jason Seaver on the television show *Growing Pains*, was a loyal fan of the Kings and had a long-standing friendship with Wayne Gretzky.

The two first met at the 1981 All-Star Game in Los Angeles, which was the first of 20 appearances Gretzky would make at the showcase. Thicke was producing that first gala dinner and was soon mentoring Gretzky on his public appearances, as his newfound fame as an NHL sensation began leading to guest spots on TV shows such as *Saturday Night Live*.

In 1988 Gretzky and his wife, Janet, were at the Canadian actor's Los Angeles home when the Oilers star got the call from Kings owner Bruce McNall that the trade was done. The newlyweds were keeping an eye on Thicke's son, Robin.

It was Robin, 11 years old at the time, who answered the phone when McNall called. His chart topper "Blurred Lines" was released in 2013, 25 years after the trade.

Alan Thicke, 69, suffered a fatal heart attack on December 13, 2016. He was playing hockey with his youngest son, Carter, at the time.

about to change. Salaries rose, and players started to move regularly, often chasing the best deal. Loyalty was a thing of the past. If Gretzky could be traded, anybody could.

Gretzky was reportedly making $1 million a season with the Oilers, with bonuses, when he was traded—a pittance on today's pay scale. He signed an eight-year, $20 million deal with the Kings.

"It was a pretty sad day in my life," then–general manager Glen Sather said in a 2013 documentary produced by the NHL Network. He had told Gretzky before the announcement that he would put a halt to the deal if that's what the superstar wanted. Gretzky said it was too late, that too much had happened. He'd heard he was being shopped around days after the Stanley Cup victory. And he had listened to Pocklington malign him during a phone conversation with McNall. His time as the Oilers' maestro was over.

"We had done everything we could do in the NHL at that time. We thought we had our team in a position to keep going for a few more years," Sather said. "To lose somebody like Wayne was pretty devastating."

It was another story in Los Angeles, where going to hockey games became hip for celebrities, with the likes of producer Jerry Bruckheimer becoming a season-ticket holder following the trade. Tom Hanks and Tom Cruise were spotted at games. Even President Ronald Reagan and his wife, Nancy, bought tickets. Such was the stature of Gretzky. Earlier that summer, a *USA Today* poll had named him the fourth-greatest athlete of all time—behind Babe Ruth, Jim Thorpe, and Muhammad Ali, and ahead of Larry Bird, Magic Johnson, Jack Nicklaus, and Reggie Jackson.

Gretzky said he went to Los Angeles to win a Stanley Cup, not to grow hockey, but he did. He was on the cover of *Sports Illustrated*, alongside Magic Johnson; a guest on *The Tonight Show with Jay Leno*. His image was on 55 million labels of Campbell's Soup, and he was featured in a Coke commercial that aired during a Super Bowl.

The Kings were selling out games by 1993, and for the first time in franchise history, they needed to set up a community-relations department. It also didn't hurt that Michael Eisner, then Disney's chief executive officer, was a fan of the game, which led to the release of the movie *The Mighty Ducks*. In 1993 Disney's Mighty Ducks of Anaheim were added to the NHL's fold.

"The very first game I played in L.A. was on a Saturday night, an exhibition game, and we had 9,000 there.... I remember in the warmup thinking, *Oh my gosh, this is going to be a lot of work.* 'Cause in Edmonton, we sold out every game with season tickets," Gretzky told CBC's Peter Mansbridge during an interview on *The National*. "I was thinking, *Oh my gosh, what have I got myself into?*

"Now when I pick up a paper periodically and I'll see on a Friday night that the Ducks have 17,000 people, and I read the same paper and the Kings are at 18,000...[that's] 35,000, 36,000 people, on the same night, going to an NHL hockey game. I go, 'Wow, this is pretty good.'"

In 1990–91 USA Hockey had 195,125 registered players. By 2012–13 that number had skyrocketed to 510,279. A year after the Kings advanced to the 1993 Stanley Cup, the Minnesota North Stars relocated to Dallas, and hockey took root in the southwest.

"Really, I think that a lot of what we see today, the success of USA Hockey and the growth of USA Hockey, really has its origins in Gretzky coming to the States and creating an awareness of the game that simply didn't exist before," said Reggie Hall, president of the Texas Amateur Hockey Association.

Fast-forward to 2014 and the Stadium Series between the Kings and the Ducks at a sold-out Dodger Stadium—an event that would have been implausible in 1988. And in 2016 Austin Matthews, who was raised in Scottsdale, Arizona, was drafted first overall by the Toronto Maple Leafs. "If you would have said that 30 years ago, nobody would have believed you," Gretzky continued in his interview with Mansbridge. "We would have all said, 'Yeah, sure.'"

Matthews, born a year after the NHL relocated to Arizona, was first exposed to hockey at a Coyotes game. He went on to play youth hockey and trained in Arizona right up until he moved to USA Hockey's National Team Development Program at age 16. He was the seventh US-born player drafted first overall, the first since the Chicago Blackhawks selected Patrick Kane in 2007.

Back in Edmonton, just prior to the start of the 2016–17 season, things shifted again. The beloved son finally returned. Gretzky was named partner and vice chairman of the Oilers Entertainment Group.

"What Wayne means to the Oilers, the NHL, and all sports, none of us can deny," said owner Daryl Katz. "We always felt the Edmonton Oilers were his home, and without question to all of us, this is where Wayne should be. This is a day that's been a long time coming."

10 Of Moose and Men

The piercing stare was Mark Messier's hallmark. Menacing and intimidating when leveled at opponents, it was the kind of look that could also stop a teammate cold...or inspire him in a game's tougher minutes.

Messier was a leader throughout his Hall of Fame career. He pushed the Oilers to a Stanley Cup in 1990, then four years later led the New York Rangers to their first championship in 54 years. No other player in the NHL has captained two different teams to Cup victories. "He's a leader with several exclamation points behind it," former Boston Bruins star Ray Bourque once said. "He's decisive, dynamic, powerful, and stubborn too. A real winner."

Messier was twice named the league's most valuable player, twice he was the players' choice for MVP. He collected five Stanley Cups in Edmonton, another in New York, and closed his career with 1,887 points in 1,756 games. Only Wayne Gretzky registered more points, and only Gordie Howe played more games.

He was a power forward with size and ferocity and skill. "Mark could burn you with his speed, bop you with his stick or drop his gloves and beat you with his fists, just like Gordie Howe," former Oilers teammate Dave Hunter once told the *Edmonton Journal*. "I ask you, where do you find another player in our day like Mark Messier? You don't."

They called him the Moose in Edmonton, where he pushed the Oilers to their fifth Stanley Cup after Wayne Gretzky was dealt to the Los Angeles Kings. He was the Messiah in New York after he boldly guaranteed victory for the Rangers in Game 6 of the 1994 Eastern Conference Finals against New Jersey. Messier then proceeded to deliver a hat trick to secure the win. The Rangers went on to claim their first Stanley Cup championship in 54 years that spring. "Come on, who does that?" former Rangers goalie Glenn Healy once asked.

Doug Messier—Mark's father—racked up 975 penalty minutes in 487 games with Edmonton and Portland in the Western Hockey League. He then instilled that tenacity, that mean streak, in his son, whose first steps in the game were in St. Albert, a city lying on Edmonton's northwestern outskirts.

When Gretzky was moved from the Indianapolis Racers to the World Hockey Association Oilers, Messier, then 17, took his spot in the indifferent state of Indiana, where the team folded 25 games into the 1978–79 season. He ended up with the Cincinnati Stingers, scoring just one goal in the WHA, but the Oilers saw enough to make him their second choice in the 1979 draft.

By 1981–82 Messier had put away 50 goals, and then was a force in the Oilers' first Stanley Cup victory in 1984, racking up 26 points and claiming the Conn Smythe Trophy as the playoff MVP. "He has to go down as one of the best all-time leaders in any professional sport," former Oilers coach John Muckler told ESPN.

Messier, who assumed the captaincy when Gretzky was moved, was at his best in the 1990 conference finals against the Chicago Blackhawks, scoring twice and adding a pair of assists in the pivotal fourth game. His heroics evened the series 2–2 and propelled Edmonton into a championship win over the Boston Bruins. "He did everything you wanted of a great player," Muckler said of that game against the Blackhawks. "It was the best game I ever saw him play as an Oiler."

The city had its chance to say thanks for the memories on February 27, 2007, when his No. 11 went up into the rafters, rightfully taking its place alongside banners belonging to Paul Coffey, Grant Fuhr, Jari Kurri, Al Hamilton, and Gretzky.

Messier skated out through a cloud of smoke, with the Stanley Cup raised over his shoulders, along with 14 of his former teammates there for the tribute. Sadly, the celebratory vibe was dampened by the trade of winger Ryan Smyth to the New York Islanders earlier in the day. Oilers general manager Kevin Lowe was to speak that night, but instead he had head coach Craig MacTavish stand in, knowing his presence would only rile the crowd after trading Smyth, a hardworking fan favorite whose contract negotiations had stalled.

Messier said later that night that the trade was just a harsh reality of the NHL, not a reflection on Smyth, and he certainly didn't fault Lowe for his absence. Spoken like a quintessential captain.

11 The Next One?

He is the beacon of hope in a city where fans have suffered through the perpetual failures of a franchise. He is also the first generational player to grace the NHL stage since Sidney Crosby—which is noteworthy given that the last time the Oilers were in the playoffs was also the year that Crosby made his debut with the Pittsburgh Penguins.

Connor McDavid, gifted with the kind of exceptional talent capable of transforming a franchise, was the windfall after the Oilers won the draft lottery in the spring of 2015. With his blazing speed, soft hands and pull-you-out-of-your-seat play-making skills, McDavid expeditiously demonstrated he was ready for the task of reviving the hockey club. In spite of a broken left clavicle—which he suffered in his 13th game in the NHL when he crashed into the end boards under the weight of Philadelphia Flyers Brandon Manning and Michael Del Zotto—McDavid closed out his abbreviated rookie season with 48 points (16 goals and 32 assists) in 45 games.

He followed that up the with a league-leading 100 points to capture the Art Ross Trophy as the NHL's scoring champion, edging out goals leader (44) Crosby and the Chicago Blackhawks' Patrick Kane (34 goals, 89 points), while propelling the Oilers to their first playoff appearance since 2006.

So outstanding was his 2016–17 season that he was also awarded the Ted Lindsay Trophy and the Hart Memorial Trophy. He was the third youngest player in league history to win the Hart, following Crosby (2007) and Gretzky (1980), who both won at the age of 19, and the first Oiler to win it since Mark Messier in 1990.

McDavid, who netted 30 regular-season goals while registering 70 assists in his sophomore season—the only player to reach the 100-point plateau—went into the postseason with a 14-game point streak. It was the longest point streak in the NHL in the 2016–17 season and the longest by an Oiler since 1987–88.

He may indeed be the Next One.

"Sid is still the best player in hockey. That's a mantle you earn over time," Wayne Gretzky told ESPN's Craig Custance during McDavid's superb sophomore season. "It's one of those things where you have to earn that title.

"Is Connor a great player? Absolutely. Does Connor have an opportunity to be the next Crosby? Absolutely. Right now, Sidney deserves to be known as the best player in the game. He's been the best player consistently in his career." Gretzky, of course, was the cornerstone of the Oilers' championship teams of the 1980s and the team captain for five seasons, from 1983 to 1988.

McDavid became the 15th player to lead the Oilers, the youngest captain in NHL history, when he was presented with the *C* a week before the start of his sophomore season. In spite of his youthfulness and his shortened first season, his teammates were certain he was ready to take the lead. "It seems the more important the game, the better he plays, and that's the kind of guy we want to follow," said veteran Matt Hendricks. McDavid, who may be as humble as he is skillful, also captained Team North America at the 2016 World Cup of Hockey.

"He has a presence, just walking through the room. People look for him, look at him," said former Chicago Blackhawks winger Kris Versteeg. "It's how it is with top guys. People want to follow Connor."

Following a game against the New York Rangers, goaltender Henrik Lundqvist was among those singing the sophomore's praises. He pointed to McDavid's lightning-quick speed, his vision, and his ability to make something happen every time he was on the ice.

The whiz kid, driven by the need to be the best, said that one of his earliest lessons from his dad was that he needed to keep skating with the puck rather than slowing down. "It's definitely a hard thing to do," McDavid once told *Sports Illustrated*. "A lot of guys, when they get the puck, they like to slow down and look for the easy play. When I get the puck, I like to speed up and put the defender in an awkward spot."

"The ability to play at full speed and still make plays is special. You've got to really be on when he's out there," San Jose Sharks defenseman Justin Braun said during the first round of the 2017 Stanley Cup playoffs.

"You never know when he's going to break out, so every night you've got to be on because he's got that ability to turn it on. Not many hockey players, when I watch them, do I go, 'Wow.' But this kid? He's something special," said Chicago Blackhawks veteran Marian Hossa. "Fun to watch."

Who knows? Perhaps McDavid is the next Great One.

12 First Time for Everything

Expectations? Yes, there have been a few heaped upon the shoulders of Connor McDavid—McJesus, as some of his online followers prefer. Before he'd even played his first game, Rogers Communications, one of the NHL's broadcasters, launched an ad campaign that was built around the 18-year-old.

The annual fall scrimmage, pitting the Oilers rookies and the University of Alberta Golden Bears, was moved from the 2,700-seat Clare Drake campus arena to Rexall Place to accommodate the curious. More than 14,000 fans showed up just to catch a glimpse of McDavid. He didn't disappoint.

Twelve games into his NHL career, he had five goals and seven assists. When he returned to the Oilers lineup three months later, after suffering a fractured clavicle, he wasted no time picking up where he'd left off. And his wizardry only accelerated in his sophomore campaign.

"Every now and then a superhero comes along in hockey, and we got one again," Bob Cole, *Hockey Night in Canada*'s storied broadcaster, told the *Globe and Mail*. "And he's in Edmonton. Just like the '80s."

Naturally, it didn't take McDavid long to establish many of his career firsts. Here's a quick rundown of some of the highlights:

First Game, October 8, 2015: Skating out between Taylor Hall and Anton Slepyshev for the season opener against the St. Louis Blues, McDavid would have preferred a much different outcome in his first NHL game. Instead, he left with two shots on net, no points, and a noticeable degree of frustration following the 3–1 loss.

He did say he'd remember his first NHL milestone for some time but that he was glad it was over, given all the attention it had been paid.

It was hardly an ordinary debut. Sportsnet broadcast the morning skate then dedicated one camera to McDavid's every move during the game. Media from around North America descended upon the Scottrade Center to document the rookie's first steps.

"He's working really hard to be himself and fit in; he doesn't want to be special, he doesn't want to be treated any differently. But he obviously is," said head coach Todd McLellan.

First Goal, October 13, 2015: In his third NHL game, McDavid tipped in his first NHL goal, a second-period marker that beat Dallas Stars goaltender Kari Lehtonen.

"I was excited, but a lot of it was relief," McDavid said after the 4–2 loss at the American Airlines Center. "It's just the pressure out there these days."

First Multipoint Game, October 17, 2015: It was a breakout game, with an exclamation point. In his first appearance in the Battle of Alberta, in a game that was broadcast on *Hockey Night in Canada*, McDavid put away two goals and registered an assist in a 5–2 win over the Calgary Flames. All that stood between the rookie and his first hat trick that night was a ridiculous Jonas Hiller paddle save.

First Choice to Wear the C: To hear his teammates and coaches tell it, McDavid cemented his claim on the captaincy when he returned from his broken collarbone in his rookie season. On October 5, 2016, the Oilers officially christened him their team leader. At 19 years and 266 days he also became the youngest captain in NHL history—by 20 days. Gabriel Landeskog was 19 years, 286 days when the Colorado Avalanche bestowed him with the title.

"That first game back he showed that he was ready to take charge," said McLellan. "He was confident [with] the way he carried himself in the locker room, the way he interacted with his teammates, through some of the meetings at the end of the season.... At that point it was real evident he was ready to lead this group."

First Game Against Sidney Crosby: McDavid has long idolized Crosby, which only added to the hype surrounding the meeting of the league's franchise centers on November 8, 2016, in Pittsburgh.

"Obviously he's the best player in the world," said McDavid prior to the game. "If you can have half his success or even a quarter of his success, I think that's a pretty amazing career.

"You know what he's been able to do and all the championships he's won. He's won basically everything there is to win. So definitely he's a pretty good guy to try and follow."

Crosby passed the compliments right back. "I think just [McDavid's] speed stands out the most...that allows him to do so many other things. He sees the ice really well, he's strong on the puck, but I think just his hockey sense and his speed are probably the biggest things."

Crosby won the first faceoff—the opening faceoff—but was held off the score sheet in a 4–3 Pittsburgh win. McDavid, who faced his counterpart shift after shift, finished with three assists.

First Hat Trick: After going 10 games without a goal and with his team on a five-game losing streak, McDavid registered his first hat trick in a 5–2 win over the Dallas Stars on November 19, 2016. His first went in off a defenseman's stick. "Three pretty lucky goals," McDavid said. "It's a funny league that way. You get grade-A chances and they're not going in, then all of a sudden, you start putting it there, and they are going in.... Definitely happy to get off that slump."

It was his 64th game in the NHL and it was in American Airlines Center in Dallas, which is where he scored his first NHL goal.

First Piece of NHL Hardware: After amassing 100 points in 2016–17, McDavid, 20, became the third-youngest player to win the Art Ross Trophy. Only Sidney Crosby and Wayne Gretzky were younger.

Gretzky was the last Oiler to win the scoring title, winning seven straight from 1980–81 through 1986–87.

13. 1 + 1 + 1 = A Lotto Luck

As improbable as it may have been, the Oilers snared the first pick overall in four of the six entry drafts staged between 2010 and 2015. And it wasn't just that the Oilers were repeatedly finishing well back of the playoff contenders, putting them in the lottery pool. Luck was also involved. A "lotto" luck.

Take the scenario that unfolded on April 18, 2015. The Oilers went into the lottery with the third-best odds (11.5 percent) after finishing 28th out of 30 teams, yet they still beat the Buffalo Sabres and Phoenix Coyotes to secure the No. 1 pick—and with it, the right to draft teenage phenom Connor McDavid. This after the Oilers had selected Nail Yakupov first overall in 2012, Ryan Nugent-Hopkins in 2011, and Taylor Hall in 2010.

"They've got some luck," Toronto Maple Leafs general manager Brendan Shanahan said at the 2015 lottery. "Obviously everybody came here today hoping to get the gold ticket. The odds were stacked against most teams." All seven Canadian teams missed the playoffs in 2015, and all were in the draft lottery.

"It's a game changer for the franchise," said Craig MacTavish, who at the time was the general manager of the franchise. "It gives the Oilers a real shot in the arm going forward.

"There's been a lot of pain and suffering, for sure, for Oiler fans, but this is a real special moment," MacTavish continued.

"There's been some pretty lean times over the last number of years but this is going to go a long way to ending that."

First introduced to the NHL in 1995, the lottery—a complexity of weighted computations and peppy Ping-Pong balls—has been refined over the years, including an adjustment in 2015 allowing all 14 non-playoff teams a chance to move up to the No. 1 spot. In 2016 the top three slots were determined by the lottery, rather than just the first overall selection.

"When you have an 80 percent chance of losing something, you have to be ready for that and think that's probably going to be the case. And that was the case," a frustrated Buffalo Sabres general manager Tim Murray said after the 2015 lottery. His Sabres went into that lottery with the best odds (20 percent) and left with the second pick. It was the second straight year Buffalo finished last in the standings and did not win the lottery.

"Thankfully it's a short drive from Buffalo. I'd hate like hell to be flying across the country to take part in it," Murray said, adding that he wasn't disappointed in the prospect of selecting Jack Eichel with the second pick, but with the process of the lottery itself.

14 An Endearing Link to the Past

If Wayne Gretzky is Edmonton's adopted son, Joey Moss is the city's cherished progeny. Moss has spent more than three decades filling water bottles, folding towels, and warming the hearts of fans as well as all the players who have passed through the dressing room doors.

"He's the one guy I really miss," forward Andrew Cogliano said following his trade to the Anaheim Ducks. "When you'd

Scene Stealer

Given his lineage, maybe it should come as no surprise that Joey Moss would be so comfortable in the spotlight.

He was onstage at the age of five, with a ukulele in hand, drawing applause for his role in the family band. His late parents, Sophie and Lloyd, fostered music in their children—all 13 of them—and eventually the Moss family was on tour, traveling to Yellowknife and Whitehorse, assuming the name the Alaska Highway Birthquakes.

have a bad game or if something happened on the ice, you'd come in and look at him, or hang out with him, and everything would be okay again. He's really special, and I really did enjoy being around him."

Moss, who has Down syndrome, won Gretzky over when the hockey star was dating his sister, Vicki. Gretzky not only convinced the Oilers to let Moss work with the equipment staff, he assisted the family in other ways. He gave Joey's widowed mom a job sorting his fan mail and established a trust fund, which by 2007 led to the opening of Joey's Home, a $1.5 million, 12-unit facility for people with physical and developmental disabilities.

After Joey had settled into his role with the Oilers, Gretzky encouraged the Edmonton Eskimos of the Canadian Football League to hire him as a locker room attendant, keeping him busy in the summer months. Joey Moss did the rest.

"We didn't know what he could do, and he just developed into a guy who was also working around the room," said Lyle Kulchisky, the Oilers' longtime equipment manager who took Moss under his wing. "I was so ignorant to Down syndrome, but getting to know Joey changed my whole view."

Over the years, Moss has become the endearing link to the Oilers of old, collecting a long list of accolades along the way. In the final game played at Rexall Place, a ceremonial banner was dropped down from the rafters and handed to Moss. He raised the banner above his head, like he was hoisting a wrestling title belt, reveling in the moment. Months later, he was front and center again when Rogers Place opened, for the ceremonial puck drop. In 2003 he received the NHL Alumni Association's Seventh Man Award for his behind-the-scenes efforts, and it was none other than Gretzky who presented the trophy. The Joey Moss Cup, an intersquad scrimmage, has been staged during the course of numerous training camps, and a larger-than-life mural of Moss decorates an exterior wall at 7016 99th Street. In 2015 Joey Moss was inducted into the Alberta Sports Hall of Fame in the Achievement category, further cementing his stature in the city.

"At one time I was known as Vicki Moss' younger brother. Now I'm known as Joey Moss' younger brother," said Stephen, who is also Joey's guardian. The two brothers are the youngest of Sophie and Lloyd Moss' 13 children. "I'm just touched by how much the organization has supported him and included him in any of the special moments for that arena."

Joey, an enthusiastic anthem singer and wrestling fan, cabs to the rink on game days, naps there after the morning skate, then settles into his seat to watch the game. Afterward, he cleans up the benches, helps with the laundry, and eventually heads home with one of the players or a member of the training staff.

Joey, who turned 53 in 2016, even postponed hernia surgery in 2006 so he could see the Oilers' playoff run through to the end.

15 The King of Kings

Flip back the pages in the history book, back to a time when the Oil Kings were Edmonton's hockey heroes. The team first took root in 1950, under the sponsorship of Jim Christiansen, owner of the Waterloo Mercury car dealership and financial backer of the Olympic medalist hockey team of the same name.

Home for the Oil Kings was the 6,000-seat Edmonton Gardens, which was usually full on Sundays. It was the one day the team couldn't sell tickets, in accordance with the Lord's Day Act, so fans would just toss coins into the silver collection.

Over the years, the rosters were rife with players capable of propelling the team to the Memorial Cup championship, many of whom moved on to the NHL. Rookies were once paid $100 a month, third-year players $150, and on January 21, 1962, the Oil Kings became the first hockey team in western Canada to have a game televised.

It was in 1954, with Norm Ullman, Johnny Bucyk, and Gerry Melnyk in the lineup, that the Oil Kings made their first trip to the junior championship, falling to the St. Catharines Teepees in the best-of-seven finals. They returned to the Memorial Cup in 1960, and again in each of the next three years, finally claiming their first title in 1963. And it was not without contention. By the time the Oil Kings and the Niagara Falls Flyers met in Game 5, in a series contested in Edmonton, there was plenty of ill will.

"In my book, they should cancel the whole thing," columnist Hal Pawson wrote in the *Edmonton Journal* after the Flyers won the fifth game by a score of 5–2. "It's gone beyond a joke. Grown men have turned hypocrites, hockey players are bashing each other over the head, and visiting fans have flipped their lids."

Flyers coach Hap Emms wanted Oil King Gregg Pilling banned from hockey after he hit defenseman Rich Morin over the head with his stick. Morin was concussed and needed a dozen stitches to close his wound, and Emms wasn't done, calling the Oil Kings dirty and the Edmonton Gardens "a sticking barn." "If they want the cup that bad they can have it," Emms said. "My players can't go on the way things are going right now and risk the chance of being crippled for life."

A casualty list was even published to chronicle the list of the battered and bruised. Two of the Flyers were out with broken legs, two had concussions, and three had a combined total of 32 stitches. There were three black eyes and a player suffering from torn stomach muscles in addition to a charley horse and badly stretched rib muscles. The Kings? Only Pat Quinn had been in the medical room, to have four facial stitches. He had broken Gary Dornhoefer's leg with a check he delivered in Game 3.

That nastiness obviously didn't leave Quinn's game. He was an intimidating presence in the NHL and even harkened back to those days during the absurdity that was the 2009–10 Oilers season. Quinn, then the Oilers' head coach, was rather indignant that one of his players didn't channel that old-school western justice after Sheldon Souray was rammed into the boards by the Calgary Flames' Jarome Iginla. "I don't understand the players of today. If that had happened in the old days, he would have got hit over the head with a stick," Quinn said. "That's the way you deal with it. In the era I come from, you're supposed to do dirt with dirt."

Quinn, who passed away in 2014 at the age of 71; Glen Sather; Pilling; Bob Falkenberg; Roger Bourbonnais; Doug Fox; and Butch Paul were among those on the Oil Kings roster in 1963. The Flyers had Terry Crisp and Bill Goldsworthy, who would go on to play in the NHL, and Bob "Butch" Barber, who moved on to the American Hockey League and the World Hockey Association.

The Oil Kings ended the drama in the following game, with a 4–3 decision and a 4–2 series victory. It was their fifth appearance in the Memorial Cup in the team's 12-year history. "It was a minute of which all Edmonton, and all Alberta, can be forever proud," wrote Pawson, days after calling for the cancellation of the series. "It was the epitome of everything that is wonderful about true sport and sportsmanship." The Oil Kings were regulars at the junior championship over the next three years, winning it all again in 1966.

Ten years later, with the Oilers of the World Hockey Association elbowing them aside on the city's sports landscape, the team was moved to Portland, becoming the Winterhawks. Former Oil Kings owner Bill Hunter looped back around again for another go with junior hockey in 1978, but that bid failed and the team was sold and moved to Montana.

Almost two decades later, the WHL returned in the form of the Edmonton Ice. Relegated to playing in the Northlands AgriCom, and unable to shake the shadow cast by Peter Pocklington's perpetual threats to move his Edmonton Oilers without more corporate support, the team was relocated to Kootenay in 1998. When the Oilers changed ownership hands, the addition of a WHL team became a priority that came to fruition on March 16, 2006, when the WHL granted Edmonton an expansion franchise.

The Oil Kings' storied past was revisited on opening night, September 20, 2007, with about 60 former players on hand for the festivities. Seven years later, the Oil Kings claimed the WHL championship and returned to the Memorial Cup, bowing out after posting a 1–2 record in the round-robin in 2012.

On May 25, 2014, they wouldn't be denied, defeating the Guelph Storm and securing the third national championship in franchise history. "It's an amazing feeling to be part of the resurgence of the Oil Kings in Edmonton," said Steve Hamilton, who was the Oil Kings' assistant coach before taking over as head coach for the 2014–15 season. His father, Al, played on the team that won the championship in 1966, upsetting Bobby Orr and the Oshawa Generals in a best-of-seven series at Toronto's Maple Leaf Gardens.

16 Playoffs Were Coffey's Stage

An extraordinary skater with the puck-handling skills of the prodigious Bobby Orr, Paul Coffey was perfectly suited for the Oilers' fast, wide-open style of play. He outscored most forwards, was a masterful quarterback, and on April 2, 1986, in a game against the Vancouver Canucks, he broke Orr's 11-year-old record of 46 goals in a season by a defenseman. Coffey matched the record late in the opening period, when a pass deflected in off defenseman Doug Halward. The record-setting goal, fittingly, came off an end-to-end rush. "I don't care if somebody gets 150 points someday and beats me, to me he's the greatest defenseman who ever played," Coffey said of his idol, who sent a congratulatory telegram.

There were many congratulations in order, of course, before Coffey retired. The same season he broke Orr's record, he registered at least a point in 28 straight games (a record that still stands), and he went on to finish the 1986 season with 48 goals (certainly a standard that will never be matched). And during the 1985 playoffs, he was a towering presence. He put up 37 points in 18 games, setting records for most goals by a defenseman in a playoff year (12), most assists (25), most assists in one game (5), most points (37), and most points in one game (6).

Hurt in the series against the Chicago Blackhawks, he had to have his left hip frozen before the games, and he later said his foot was cracked, but it didn't seem to hamper his impact. "And the back? Well, it's just sore as hell, and getting hit by Brian Propp didn't help any," he said at the end of the series against the Philadelphia Flyers. Propp sent Coffey into a goal post, but he bounced back and scored two key goals, including the game winner. Later that spring, he won the first of three Norris Trophies he'd collect during a career that saw him register 1,531 points in 1,409 games (396 goals, 1,135 assists). One year earlier, Coffey had finished second in league scoring with 126 points but lost out in the Norris voting to Rod Langway, who had nine goals and 33 points.

"He was a great player and a solid defenseman," Coffey said of Langway to Postmedia's Michael Traikos years later. "Rod deserved the Norris Trophy, but it is harder to get up the ice and compete and be offensive than it is the other way. The other way is just commitment.

"If you didn't score, you didn't get paid. It's just how it was back then. But if I had known that blocking shots and dumping pucks around the boards would give me $5 million a year, maybe I would have done it more."

17 The Great Goal Gaffe

Years after Steve Smith's errant clearing pass ended up in the Oilers' net, his teammates were still pointing to the fact that there were almost 15 minutes left to play, that there was time for the team to right his wrong, that it wasn't all on his shoulders. Talk about bizarre playoff moments would not be complete without a mention of that fateful play that unfolded in the 1986 playoffs against the Calgary Flames in front of 17,498 incredulous fans at Northlands Coliseum.

It was Game 7 of the Smythe Division Finals, and when the rookie defenseman saw Calgary's Lanny McDonald bearing down, he tried to make a pass up the middle from behind his own net. Instead, the puck hit the back of goaltender Grant Fuhr's left leg and bounced in, ending the Oilers' quest for their third consecutive Stanley Cup.

Perry Berezan, who dumped the puck in and was already on his way to the Flames' bench, got credit for the goal. Smith, who turned 23 that day, was devastated. "It was human error," a teary-eyed Smith said that night. "I guess I'll have to live with it."

"It's a tough position for someone that young and promising to be in," teammate Randy Gregg said. "It would be tough for a 10-year veteran."

Smith was tied to the bench after his gaffe, but he bravely faced the media that night. He also found a dose of atonement a year later, asserting himself in the postseason—a contribution not lost on Wayne Gretzky, who handed the defenseman the Stanley Cup after the Oilers had defeated the Philadelphia Flyers.

"If I think for one second people are not going to remember, I'm a fool to think that," Smith told the *Calgary Sun* 25 years later.

"Everyone talks about the Steve Smith goal—well, they forget it was a seven-game series," McDonald said when he looked back on the 1986 playoff series. "We had to find a way to win three other games. If that [had] happened in Game 3 or 4, no one would be talking about it. They'd be talking about what an unbelievable series it was. And it was."

By the time his playing career ended in 2001, Smith had logged 804 regular-season games plus another 134 in the postseason, playing for Edmonton, the Chicago Blackhawks, and the Flames.

He also weathered all the full-throated pleas for him to shoot the puck when the Oilers were in the Saddledome—at least until he responded...in his own way. In a preseason game in 1990, the crowd was at it again whenever Smith had the puck. "Shoot! Shoot!" they yelled. This time he obliged, lobbing a puck toward Oilers goaltender Bill Ranford. "I told Billy a couple of days ago that if we were up a goal, or playing well, to be ready; I was going to fire it back to him," said Smith. "And for God's sake, don't let it in!"

"We talked about it before the game," said Ranford. "I was just a little surprised that it was that early. I thought maybe he might give me a nod or something—but he didn't."

18 The Cup Runneth Away

The 1987 Stanley Cup Finals that featured another matchup between the Oilers and the Philadelphia Flyers evolved into an epic showdown on the ice, with the dogged Flyers pushing the series to seven games. Goaltender Ron Hextall, in particular, was so good that when it was over, he was named the most valuable player, a distinction typically reserved for a player on the championship team.

But there was some cagey psychological play unfolding off the ice too. With his team down 3–1 in the series, Flyers head coach Mike Keenan contacted the NHL's director of security and asked to borrow the Stanley Cup prior to Game 5. He wanted to display the trophy in the dressing room, to motivate his players—a particularly unusual request given the superstitions attached to the coveted Cup. "That really surprised me," the NHL's Frank Torpey said. "That's the first time in the 17 years I've been with the league that a coach has asked for the Stanley Cup. He's going against tradition. Most people playing in the Stanley Cup Finals don't want to see the Cup around because they're superstitious."

To emphasize his point, Torpey relayed a tale about an exchange he had had with the Boston Bruins' president, Weston Adams, in 1972. When he told Adams the Cup had to be stored in the Garden because the series was on the verge of ending, Adams told him he didn't want "that thing" in the building. He told Torpey that if he was going to bring it into the building, he did not want to know about it.

Keenan, meanwhile, had no such reservations. With the Flyers facing elimination, he wanted his players to touch the prize they were chasing. To note its history, its grandeur. So it was wheeled into the room. And Philadelphia won 4–3. After the skate on the morning of Game 6, Keenan had the Cup removed from its crate once again, closing the room off to everyone but the players and team officials. "Actually some of us were throwing tape balls into the Cup to see if we could score some baskets," said Rick Tocchet. "I think it was nice to see the Cup, but really it doesn't do anything for me. It just tries to show you what's at stake. [But] if you're not motivated by now, you never will be."

Nevertheless, the Flyers won Game 6 by a score of 3–2, so naturally Keenan wanted the trophy in their room before the final game. It was nowhere to be found. Oilers general manager / head coach Glen Sather had his equipment manager highjack the Cup and stash it in the trunk of his car.

"All I can say is, the Cup went missing," Lyle Kulchisky said after the Oilers had secured a 3–1 victory to win another championship. "I hear a clown from the Tarzan Zerbini Circus accidentally loaded it on his truck and it didn't make it back here until 6:05. I'm just glad it got back here in time to be presented."

When the Oilers officially got their hands on the trophy, there were two memorable moments from the on-ice celebration. First, captain Wayne Gretzky deliberately, graciously handed the trophy over to Steve Smith. A year earlier, Smith was lamenting the goal he had put into his own net, interrupting the Oilers' quest for their third-straight title.

Then, when Marty McSorley got his turn for the traditional lap around the arena, he skated over to the stands, frantically searching the sea of faces for his father. When they were united, they fell into each other's arms and cried. McSorley said at the time he wanted to thank his dad for all his support. "My dad was too nervous to watch the games from the stands, so he'd walk around this building, underneath the stands," McSorley said years later, when he was back in Edmonton for the closing of the old rink. "When we won and they opened the door and rolled out the carpet, I was almost lost because you win a Stanley Cup, and it's just bigger than life. Then there's my dad…and when he walked out on the ice, I just gave him a great big hug and said, 'We got *our* name on the Stanley Cup.'"

It was his first Stanley Cup victory, and a scene that even touched referee Dave Newell. "I've been in hockey a long time," Newell said at the time, "but when McSorley found his dad and started hugging him, and the old man's tears were just running down his cheeks…that's one of the nicest things I've ever seen in the game."

19 One More, for Old Times' Sake

The Oilers, with all their swagger and skill, had monopolized the playoff stage, winning four Stanley Cups in five years while setting all kinds of ridiculous offensive records in the process. Then Wayne Gretzky, the bedrock of the team, was ripped out of the lineup and traded to Los Angeles. No one anticipated the Oilers would bounce back and win their fifth championship, particularly not after Gretzky and his Kings knocked the club out of the 1989 playoffs. "In retrospect, that really severed the ties for all of us, because what people predicted to happen happened," Kevin Lowe once said. "Wayne Gretzky came in with another team and knocked us out. That rebooted us as a team for the following season."

"A lot of people thought we wouldn't be able to overcome losing him and what he did for us, but look at the guys we still had," defenseman Charlie Huddy said. "We just had to get through the initial shock, get over it as players and move on. It took us a bit, but that's what we ended up doing."

In 1990, just two years after Gretzky had been dealt, the Oilers defeated the Boston Bruins 4–1 to win their fifth Cup in seven years. That it took 22 games—their longest playoff run in 11 years—mattered not. "Nobody expected us to be back this soon," said Craig Simpson, who led the scoring with 16 goals that spring.

Goaltender Grant Fuhr was out with a dislocated shoulder, but his replacement, Bill Ranford, seized the moment, and the Kid Line of Martin Gelinas, Joe Murphy, and Adam Graves combined for 30 points in 22 games.

Jari Kurri, Mark Messier, Lowe, and Fuhr—future Hall of Famers all—were still with the team, as were Huddy and Randy Gregg. All seven players had been on the team for Edmonton's first Cup. Messier edged out Ray Bourque by two points to win the Hart as the league's most valuable player that year, Kurri dominated Game 2 with three goals and two assists, and Anderson scored on an end-to-end rush early in the middle frame of the fifth game, then set up Simpson with a behind-the-net pass to help put the finishing touch on the series. Ranford, who surrendered eight goals in the 18 periods he played against the Bruins, won the Conn Smythe Trophy as the playoff MVP.

Goalie Bill Ranford makes a flying kick save during the Stanley Cup Finals against the Boston Bruins.

"This is probably the nicest of the five [Cups], because coming out of training camp, we never expected to be here," said Coach John Muckler, "and we won on a good team concept and a lot of hard work."

20 First Say "Stanley," Then Say "Cheese"

It has become commonplace for the giddy, freshly crowned Stanley Cup champs to gather at center ice with their shiny prize, posing for the obligatory photo. But did you know it was a tradition that was reestablished by the Oilers?

Prior to 1988, photographers, fans, and family members would spill onto the ice surface after the Oilers' victories—certainly a crowded, chaotic scene in Edmonton given that the club won its first three championships on home ice. Then on May 26, 1988, after the Oilers had defeated the Boston Bruins 6–3 to secure their fourth Stanley Cup—again on home ice—Gretzky took the Stanley Cup, skated out to center ice, set down the prize, and proceeded to gather teammates and team staff around while the security kept the fans at bay.

"In the previous three years, it was sort of bedlam...and I can remember going into the arena before Game 4 and saying to one of the security guys, 'Please just keep everybody off the ice for a half hour so we can really enjoy it as a group,'" Gretzky said in an interview with Sportsnet's Christine Simpson. "We got that chance and that opportunity for that picture, and people said, 'Oh, you took that picture because you knew you were getting traded.' I had no idea I was going to get traded, but I just really felt like, 'Okay, this would be very cool to have this picture taken.'" And thus began a tradition that continues to this day. That Gretzky was traded less than three months later only adds to the lore. It was also the last Cup he would win.

"In my office, at my home, [that picture is] one of my prized possessions: that moment on the ice with your teammates," said Craig Simpson.

Gretzky said the idea of posing with Stanley came from grainy, decades-old images he'd once seen of the Montreal Canadiens and the Toronto Maple Leafs back in their glory years. "I remember thinking, *Wow, that would be really cool. We should do a great team picture*," Gretzky said. "We restarted history again as a team, and that's what made it special. It was a really unique group that happened to be one of the greatest teams that ever played."

21 Take a Stroll in the Hall

When Wayne Gretzky was introduced as the ambassador for the NHL's 2017 centennial celebration, he told a tale about a trip he once made to the Hockey Hall of Fame. Gretzky revels in the history that is encapsulated in the Hall, a fixation that began when he was a youngster. He spent hours staring at the exhibits that were located in Toronto's Canadian National Exhibition Stadium at the time.

Later, after the Hall found a permanent home in downtown Toronto and his fame grew, Gretzky had to maintain a degree of anonymity when he visited, which he did by perching a pair of glasses on his nose and by pulling a ball cap down over his head.

The trip Gretzky recounted in 2017 was one particular father-son visit, during which Wayne and his son were trying their hands at the interactive shooting display following a two-hour tour. His

Did You Know?

The first inductees to the Hockey Hall of Fame were inducted in 1945, but there wasn't actually a home for the game changers. Plans were under way to construct a home in Kingston, Ontario—pegged by some historians as the birthplace of hockey—but the membership failed to come up with sufficient funds. NHL president Clarence Campbell withdrew the league's support in 1958, and a decision was made to locate the Hockey Hall of Fame in Toronto.

The Hall officially opened on August 26, 1961, and was a popular stop for those taking in the Canadian National Exhibition, the annual fair on Toronto's summer calendar. There just weren't enough visitors during the rest of the year to cover the operating costs, and by the mid-1980s, it was costing the National Hockey League more than $300,000 a year to maintain the facility.

The search for a home in downtown Toronto ended with the procurement of a magnificent heritage building that was constructed in 1885, and once the head office of the Bank of Montreal. The building was renovated at a cost of $27 million, and in 1993 the Hockey Hall of Fame opened at its new location. More than 500,000 toured the state-of-the-art Hall in its first year. Several renovation and revitalization projects have since been undertaken with today's yearly visitor tally averaging at about 275,000.

As for all those early inductees—the 42 players and builders who were inducted into a homeless shrine? They were honored by the league in 1958. The first members to go in the Hockey Hall of Fame were: Dan Bain, Hobey Baker, Dubbie Bowie, Chuck Gardiner, Eddie Gerard, Frank McGee, Howie Morenz, Tommy Phillips, Harvey Pulford, Art Ross, Hod Stuart, and Georges Vezina, who went in as players. Sir Montagu Allan and Lord Frederick Stanley were the first to go into the Hall as builders.

son, fueled by his four-for-five stint, encouraged his dad to give the game a try. "I got out there and missed the first three shots I took," Wayne Gretzky said, "and the young man who was taking care of the line walked over to me and said, 'Sir, if you move your hand down the stick a little bit farther'...and I lifted my hat up, and I said, 'Go get me one of those pucks there. There's 802 up there.'

My son killed himself laughing. But I love every part of the Hall of Fame. It's heaven to me…I love it there."

Gretzky, who dominated the league's record book like no other, could have his own wing at the Hall. As it is, there's no shortage of

Did You Know, Part 2?

The Oilers have several items in their team Hall of Fame at Rogers Place that are on loan from the Hockey Hall of Fame, in addition to artifacts that the franchise collected. Among the pieces of memorabilia? A stall from the original dressing room at Rexall Place, a collection of record-setting pucks, and Wayne Gretzky's rookie jersey.

"What's great about Wayne [Gretzky] is that he sets the bar so high for donating items to the Hall of Fame. It's unbelievable," said Peter Jagla, the Hockey Hall of Fame's vice president of marketing and attractions. "And everybody else, obviously, feels an obligation to follow suit."

Almost half the material collected by the NHL's Hockey Hall of Fame is on display; the rest is rotated so the displays change frequently. One of the newer, more permanent fixtures is Franchise Alley, which highlights the stars and history of each franchise.

No More Exceptions for the Exceptional

After Wayne Gretzky was ushered into the Hockey Hall of Fame with the fanfare befitting a player of his ilk, the Hall's board of governors declared that from that point forward, players had to be retired for at least three years before they were eligible for nomination.

Inducted seven short months after his final game, Gretzky was the 10th player to go straight into the Hall without a waiting period. He followed: Aubrey Clapper (1947), Maurice Richard (1961), Ted Lindsay (1966), Leonard Kelly (1969), Terry Sawchuk (1971), Jean Beliveau (1972), Gordie Howe (1972), Bobby Orr (1979), and Mario Lemieux (1997). All had the customary waiting periods waived on the basis of "outstanding preeminence and skill."

The selection committee's vote to waive Gretzky's waiting period was unanimous, and on November 22, 1999, he was inducted along with former referee Andy van Hellemond (referee/linesman category) and Ian "Scotty" Morrison (builders category).

displays. Some were gathered from his father's basement, some from the Oilers, others from Hockey Canada. In conjunction with his induction into the Hall on November 22, 1999, the Hockey Hall of Fame opened a 2,300-square-foot exhibit dedicated to Gretzky memorabilia. It was the first and only time a player has been honored with a wing for his induction ceremony. In 2017 that wing became home to archives celebrating the NHL's 100th anniversary.

"After his last game with the Rangers, he actually handed over his entire [equipment] bag to Phil Pritchard, our curator. He literally said, 'Here, this is destined for the Hall,'" said Peter Jagla, the vice president of marketing and attractions. "[And] when we went to his dad's, Walter just said, 'Take what you want.'"

There's a long, revolving list of collectibles from the Oilers—all representing one record or another. Nothing, of course, matches Gretzky's actual accomplishments. He is the NHL's leading scorer (2,857 points), a four-time Stanley Cup champion, and when he retired, he held or co-owned 61 league records. Of those, 40 are for the regular season, 15 are for the playoffs, and 6 are tied to the All-Star Game. And in spite of the time that has passed, only a few have been eclipsed.

"I didn't expect to do what I did," Gretzky said. "My only regret is that I didn't really sit back and take it all in. I just kind of did it."

22 Mr. Freeze

His fate was sealed when he hopped up into the seat of a Zamboni in the picturesque town of Jasper, Alberta, and cleaned a sheet of ice that he had helped prep. Dan Craig was a high school student then, not the NHL's ice guru, but that job in the town arena got him started on a path that would eventually take him to Edmonton, where he would meticulously groom the ice for the Oilers for 11 seasons.

In 1997 Craig was hired by the NHL—in large part because Oilers general manager Glen Sather had been pushing for more consistency in the rinks around the league. "The puck always ran really well [in Edmonton]," Craig once said before calling attention to the long, precise passes Wayne Gretzky would make to Jari Kurri—passes Gretzky wouldn't always try on the road if he wasn't as sure of the ice surface. "The players told us when the ice was really good," Craig continued, "and we just took all the numbers from all the charts from that particular time and…would try to duplicate them every single day."

One of Craig's first noteworthy projects for the NHL was the installation of a rink atop a swimming pool in the Yoyogi National Gymnasium in Tokyo in advance of two regular-season games between the Vancouver Canucks and the Mighty Ducks of Anaheim.

Since then, he's had his fingerprints all over the ice that has played host to all the outdoor games—including the league's first regular-season outdoor game between the Oilers and Montreal Canadiens in front of 57,167 fans on a bitterly cold and windy afternoon in Edmonton's Commonwealth Stadium.

He's put ice in Chicago's Wrigley Field, and he saw to the installation of a rink in Los Angeles' sun-baked Dodger Stadium, but as the league's senior director of facilities operations, Craig's scope is much broader than aluminum ice trays, portable refrigeration systems, and weather reports. He's worked the Olympic games in addition to supervising the crews at all 31 arenas. He was summoned to the Barclays Center in Brooklyn the year the New York Islanders' new home opened, and he was in Edmonton before Rogers Place opened.

"He turned the science of making great ice in Edmonton into something that could be taken elsewhere," said Trent Evans, who worked on Craig's crew in Edmonton. "Everything from what the Zamboni drivers did to the water to the temperature of the water. He really turned it into a science."

The first outdoor rink Craig ever made was a backyard rink for his two sons in the town of Bonnyville, 240 kilometers northeast of Edmonton. One of those sons, Mike, embraced the family craft and has since worked in Edmonton and elsewhere alongside his father, the Ice Man.

Dan Craig was once quoted as saying, "For me, I don't care if you're making $9 million a year or you're nine years old, you're going to get the best of whatever I can do on that particular day."

What's in a Name?

There was nothing resembling a name-the-team contest when Bill Hunter was assembling the Edmonton club that was destined for the World Hockey Association. He just elected to go with the Oilers, with the explanation that he wanted to pay homage to the oil industry—though he first registered the team as the Edmonton Oil Kings.

When the Calgary Broncos failed to come up with the $100,000 bond required to join the WHA, Hunter switched the name to the Alberta Oilers, thinking the team would play some games in both Calgary and Edmonton.

As for the logo, it was designed by an artist, but there was a reason it bore a striking resemblance to the Gulf Oil trademark with its blue-and-orange color scheme. Hunter, being the salesman he was, set up a meeting with the head of Gulf Western and sold him on a sponsorship agreement that would pay the WHA franchise $10 million just for wearing the company's colors. The deal was later overturned by the oil company's board of directors, in large part because Imperial Oil, Gulf's parent company, had ties with *Hockey Night in Canada*, Hunter relayed in his autobiography, *Wild Bill: Bill Hunter's Legendary 65 Years in Canadian Sport.*

Although he was discouraged that such a lucrative deal had evaporated, Hunter didn't wipe the slate clean. He stuck with the logo and the color scheme. And the team was renamed the Edmonton Oilers for the 1973–74 season.

24 Leaders of the Pack

Al Hamilton's ties to the game reach back to a time when Tim Horton was a teammate, not a coffee franchise. When Hamilton was with the legendary Edmonton Oil Kings, the team not only won the Memorial Cup in 1966 but knocked off Bobby Orr's Oshawa Generals to win it.

There were three Memorial Cup appearances in the career of the puck-rushing defenseman, not to mention 257 NHL games and numerous other highlights. But his enduring link to the Oilers is his captaincy. Hamilton was the undisputed leader of the franchise when it navigated the rocky road that was the WHA. He was the first captain of the franchise. "I never thought much about it when I had it," he said. "It was just what you were supposed to do, so do it. But it is an honor. It's still very significant. People will say, 'Have you met Al? He was the first captain of the Oilers.'"

Wayne Gretzky, Mark Messier, and Doug Weight are among the players who have had the distinction of wearing the *C* for the Oilers. But none were as young as Connor McDavid, who was named captain prior to the start of the 2016–17 season. He is the 15th player to lead the Oilers, the youngest to receive the honor in the NHL. "He's mature beyond his years," Oilers coach Todd McLellan said of the appointment. "He's dealt with [the media] since he was 14. He handles himself very well and takes care of his teammates in front of and with the media—which we think is very important in a Canadian franchise. He is an ambassador of the game, which I think you have to be as a captain…he understands his role."

Hamilton did too, even if the landscape has changed through the decades. "If you're going to be a leader and you're going to pipe up, you have to have credibility," he said. "The fact of the matter is that a lot of times what you do is more important than what you say. You don't have to be the best player, but you certainly have to be somebody that everybody respects."

He got no argument from Todd Marchant, who spent nine-plus seasons with the Oilers, wearing an *A* during some of those years. He was playing with the Anaheim Ducks in 2007 when the team won the Stanley Cup. It was a team laden with veterans. "Scott Niedermayer was our captain, and there's no question he was our leader because he was our best player. But he didn't have to say a lot," said Marchant. "He had guys like Chris Pronger, Sean O'Donnell, Teemu Selanne, [Jean-Sebastien] Giguere, Rob Niedermayer...we had all these guys who had 12, 13, 14 years [of] experience in the league and had probably worn an *A* or a *C* at some point in their careers, so it wasn't a big responsibility. Now don't get me wrong. When Scott would stand up and stay something, it was like, 'Okay.'

Roll Call

2016–	Connor McDavid
2015–16	No captain
2013–15	Andrew Ference
2010–13	Shawn Horcoff
2007–10	Ethan Moreau
2001–07	Jason Smith
1999–2001	Doug Weight
1995–99	Kelly Buchberger
1994–95	Shayne Corson
1992–94	Craig MacTavish
1991–92	Kevin Lowe
1988–91	Mark Messier
1983–88	Wayne Gretzky
1981–83	Lee Fogolin
1980–81	Blair MacDonald & Lee Fogolin
1979–80	Ron Chipperfield

Better Late Than Never

Al Hamilton, who wore the *C* for the Oilers in the WHA, was honored on October 10, 1980, with the official retirement of his jersey before a game against the Quebec Nordiques. The defenseman was the only player to wear No. 3 for the Oilers in the NHL and is the first captain of the franchise.

His number, however, didn't go into the rafters until April 5, 2001, after Wayne Gretzky had been honored. Theirs were the only two hanging in the rink until Jari Kurri's number was retired six months later.

"The best example of that was in Game 4 against Ottawa in the Stanley Cup Finals. Daniel Alfredsson fires the puck at Scotty. In the locker room, it was like, 'Who's going to get him?' Everybody wanted a piece of him. Scotty came in and said, 'No, that's not why we're here. We're here to win the game. Win this series. He knew what to say and when to say it to calm everything down. We went out and won that game and the series."

25 A Shrewd Eye for Talent

At Edmonton's draft table in Ottawa in 2008, one lone chair sat empty—a poignant tribute to Lorne Davis. Davis was the Godfather, the icon, the dean of deducing which young players had the tools to develop into NHL players. He passed away on December 20, 2007, at the age of 77.

For more than two decades, Lorne Davis scoured rinks for future Oilers, pushing particularly hard for Ryan Smyth and Grant Fuhr. "I made a couple of trips with him, and it was just amazing.

Everybody would gather around," said his eldest son, Darrell. "If you asked him who he was proudest of, I think it would have been Kelly Buchberger. Bucky was such a late pick...but Lorne loved the desire he had. That's where Lorne excelled, with those later selections."

Davis squeezed in 95 NHL games during a playing career that spanned a decade, winning a Stanley Cup with Montreal in 1953. When his playing days were behind him, he tried his hand at coaching, a stint that included co-coaching the 1980 Olympic team with Father David Bauer.

He started scouting in 1966, passing his passion for sport down through the family. Son Brad scouted for the Oilers until the staff was changed under general manager Peter Chiarelli, Darrell was a longtime sports reporter with the *Regina Leader-Post*, and daughter Liane has been teaching power skating to NHLers for years. Shirley Davis, the matriarch of the clan, lost her fight with cancer in 1992.

"My dad grew up in Lumsden, skating on the sloughs like Gordie Howe, and he had magazines on the floor so he could eat supper with his skates on and go back out and skate," Darrell recalled.

"I just accepted the fact that everybody was a buddy," Darrell continued. "Scotty Bowman would be phoning to talk to Lorne, college coaches would call...it was just normal to think all these guys were my dad's budd[ies].... Those roots just spread out everywhere. I think my dad knew everybody in hockey."

Davis, who joined the Oilers for the 1979–80 season, would often push management to heed his advice. He argued vehemently against the selection of Jason Bonsignore in 1994, whom the Oilers took with the fourth pick overall, but he did sway head scout Barry Fraser and general manager Glen Sather to take Smyth at No. 6.

He was also one of Glenn Anderson's advocates. Before he was drafted by the Oilers in 1979, Anderson had been tutored by Davis at a Canadian Olympic team camp in Calgary. He even spent a summer at the Davis house while attending a hockey camp in Regina. Anderson was in Ottawa to honor Davis at the 2008 NHL Entry Draft. "He was more than just a scout," Anderson said that day. "I have a real soft spot for him.... I don't know if I'll forget his stories and his smile—even though he may have told the same stories one or more times over."

"We called [Anderson] a part-time boarder," said Darrell. "He was supposed to be there every night, but I don't think he was. The Craven Big Valley Jamboree was on, and Glenn was out there a little bit...but he made it to every class he was supposed to."

If he had had his druthers, Lorne Davis would have continued to pull out his timeworn scouting reports, rather than the computer he was instructed to lug around from rink to rink. He was old-school. "When they started doing things on computers, he eventually got taught—grudgingly—how to keep track of things," said Darrell. "But when we had to clean out the house, there were still forms form the old St. Louis Blues days and the old New York Rangers days where he rated players by hand."

Lorne Davis also didn't take any holidays in the winter, and in the summer he didn't want to travel after spending the winter months on the road. Hockey games morphed into nights out with Shirley. They would attend the Regina Pats games some nights, and other nights they'd make the trek to Melville, Weyburn, Saskatoon, and Swift Current.

"[My mom] knew nothing about hockey growing up—she came from a non-sports family—but it got to the point in the off-seasons where the college coaches would be phoning to check on players, and if Lorne wasn't there, they'd talk to Shirley. Hockey was in all our blood," Darrell said.

Fittingly, at the 2008 draft, the Oilers used their first selection to take Jordan Eberle, who grew up on Janzen Crescent, five doors down from the Davises. There were countless street hockey games, up until the Eberles moved to Calgary. "It was me and

Jordan against the other eight kids on the street," said Darrell. "I didn't score many goals, but I got a lot of assists. When he scored his first [NHL] goal, he walked around Ian White and finished with a backhand. I said I saw that move—that little toe drag and backhand flip—on Janzen Crescent. And I know my dad watched him growing up. He always liked him."

26 Misery on Manchester

Daryl Evans' recollection of the first five goals the Los Angeles Kings scored in their incomparable comeback victory over the Oilers in a 1982 playoff series lacks some clarity, which has nothing to do with time and everything to do with the fact that he didn't see all the goals. Evans had been banished to the dressing room with a misconduct midway through the third period of the historic game. "A bunch of us got those 10-minute misconducts that you got for waltzing around when there was an altercation going on," he said. "We were all escorted to the locker room and didn't get back until overtime. So we just listened to it from underneath the building."

The best-of-five opening-round playoff series pitted the under-dog Kings, who closed out the regular season fourth in the division with a record of 24–41–15, against the upstart Oilers. Wayne Gretzky had racked up an improbable 92 goals and 212 points in the regular season. Glenn Anderson, Paul Coffey, Mark Messier, and Jari Kurri also had a hand in the season that saw the Oilers finish second overall with 111 points and 417 goals. Nevertheless, the Kings were not ready to concede anything. Not even when they were down 5–0 in Game 3—a game that to this day stands as one of the great playoff upsets—the Miracle on Manchester.

It was April 10, 1982, and the teams had reconvened at the Forum with one win apiece. Los Angeles had taken the opening game by a score of 10–8 with Edmonton securing a 3–2 overtime win the following night. By the second intermission, the Oilers had built a commanding 5–0 lead. Kings owner Jerry Buss left early in the third; fans too filed out. But the players refused to roll over.

Jay Wells got the Kings on the board early in the third period, Doug Smith scored on a rebound, and when Charlie Simmer rolled the puck in from behind the net to make it 5–3, there was 5:22 left on the clock.

The Oilers had their chances as the game wore on but couldn't convert, couldn't regain the momentum. With an extra attacker on the ice and only a goal separating the teams after Mark Hardy made it 5–4, Jim Fox took the puck off Gretzky.

There were just five seconds left on the clock when rookie Steve Bozek put away a rebound to send the game to overtime, setting the stage for Evans. At 2:35 of OT, he took a draw from Doug Smith and sent a shot over Grant Fuhr's shoulder. "I don't even have to close my eyes to visualize it," said Evans, the Kings' conversant radio analyst. "The one thing that I really recall is that the puck was dumped into Edmonton's zone and Grant Fuhr made a save. I remember at that moment thinking he should have put the puck down and just kept it in play.

"[Coach] Don Perry put myself and Doug Smith out for the faceoff, along with Steve Bozek—three rookies. I was lined up alongside Kevin Lowe. That was the day when you just had the one hash mark so you could put your stick in a guy's ribs and hang on to him. He could keep you at bay, but for whatever reason, I backed away from him and Doug did a great job of pulling the puck back between his legs…I just put the puck in the direction of the net. The puck had eyes. It found its way through the legs, then up over Grant's right shoulder. I caught that one with all I could.

It's something I'll never forget. It was just one of those games. It was magical."

The Kings went on to win the series, only to bow out to the Vancouver Canucks in the division final. It was a hard lesson for the young, cocky Oilers, who admitted as much when they returned to training camp.

"When you see the clips of that game, and they had the 5–0 lead, they had smiles on their faces—and rightfully so," Evans said. "They had a 5–0 lead and seemed to be completely in control of getting the series back in their favor.

"But that was an unbelievable hockey team. You look at the players they had and the ability that they had as a group. I just think it was probably the greatest thing that happened to that team. It dialed them all back in, and they went on to greatness after that.

"It was an unbelievable chapter in them becoming who they eventually became and the championships they went on to win."

27 Crowning the King on His Former Stage

It was as if a Hollywood scriptwriter had a heavy hand in the proceedings when Wayne Gretzky returned to Edmonton on October 15, 1989, in a Los Angeles Kings uniform, on the verge of supplanting Gordie Howe as the NHL's scoring leader.

A five-minute stoppage in play was in the plans, and Edmonton captains Mark Messier, Jari Kurri, and Kevin Lowe were set to make a presentation to their ex-teammate if he broke the record on his former stage. Among those on hand to witness the moment was Howe, who had been the all-time scoring leader since passing

Maurice Richard on January 16, 1960. Gretzky needed just two points to alter history.

"Wayne and I were talking this summer about it, and he said there was a good chance it would happen here in the sixth game. I remember thinking that Wayne was the only guy who'd know the

The Unsurpassable Streak

Wayne Gretzky's incomparable three-and-a-half-month point-scoring streak has often been cataloged in the same stratosphere as Joe DiMaggio's 56-game hitting streak. What might make it even more remarkable is that one season earlier he was being lauded for beating Guy Lafleur's 28-game point streak by two games.

Between October 5, 1983 (the Oilers' opening game), and January 25, 1984, Gretzky earned at least a point in 51 consecutive games, amassing 61 goals and 153 points. He scored his 50th goal of the season in Game 42. Twice, he scored eight points in a game.

In the 44th game, he scored an empty-net goal with just two seconds left on the clock. It was his only point of the game. Eight times there were only three minutes left on the clock when he secured his first point.

But with goaltender Markus Mattsson in the Kings' net and not one but two defensemen shadowing Gretzky in a game played in Edmonton, his streak ended in a 4–2 loss. "I feel bad. I was cheering for him too," said Kings coach Rogie Vachon. "It's [just] very hard to change lines against him, so I put two defensemen on against him all night, and [Jay Wells and Mark Hardy] did a tremendous job."

A week earlier, Gretzky left the ice with an injured shoulder after a heavy hit, but he didn't use it as an excuse. He just didn't step out of the lineup until after his streak ended. When he got back in the lineup, he registered points in 20 of the last 22 games, closing out the season with 87 goals and 205 points in 74 games.

"In other sports, you can miss a game and your streak will stay intact. In hockey, you miss a game and it's over," Gretzky said. "So not only do you have to perform every night, you also have to be able to battle through injury. I think I was a little lucky along the way, but I'm very proud of the record."

schedule in July," said Kings owner Bruce McNall at the time. He had acquired the league's luminary 17 months earlier in the game-changing trade with the Edmonton Oilers. "It is ironic, but it's also fair to see the fans of Edmonton be part of this."

Gretzky was a skinny 17-year-old when he first arrived in Edmonton, spending one season in the World Hockey Association before he started rewriting the NHL record book while in an Oilers uniform. He put Edmonton on the map, so it was only right that he became the league's scoring king in the Coliseum.

Being the miracle worker he was, Gretzky assisted on the game's first goal at 4:32 to tie the record, then with just 53 seconds remaining in regulation, he sent a backhand past Bill Ranford to tie the game and register his $1,851^{st}$ career point. The faithful in the building were on their feet, chanting his name, celebrating a record he set in his 11th season (Howe built his point tally over 26 seasons).

Messier presented Gretzky with a gold bracelet encrusted with 1.851 carats of diamonds; the NHL gave him an engraved silver tea tray. When the team returned to Los Angeles two days later, McNall presented him with a pot containing 1,851 gold American Eagle coins, each worth about $100 at the time, and gave Howe a pot with 1,850 silver pieces.

"I don't know how he does these things so dramatically," said Howe. "I was cheering like hell when the puck went in…. There's no sense of loss, I feel more gain than anything…I held the record for a long time."

Gretzky wasn't done, for the night however. He also scored the overtime winner. "What better way to end it than in Hollywood style," said Kings teammate Luc Robitaille. "It was unbelievable the way he did it. When you look back on it, he's scored so many great goals like that under a lot of pressure."

28 Cool Hand Fuhr

He never owned a splendid goals-against average. In fact Grant Fuhr's career average of 3.38 is the worst amongst the goaltenders who have taken up residence in the Hockey Hall of Fame. What Fuhr did have were five Stanley Cup victories from his 10 seasons with the Oilers, a stellar win-loss record, and the ability to pull off the clutch performances. If there was a big game on the line, he was on his game.

"The Oilers back then played wide-open, offensive hockey, and they abandoned Grant for periods every night and they could do it, because they knew he'd backstop them," said Mike Keenan, whose Philadelphia Flyers lost two Stanley Cups to Fuhr and the Oilers.

Fuhr won his lone Vezina Trophy as the league's best goaltender for collecting 40 wins in the 4,304 minutes he played during the 1987–88 season. It was a strong enough season that he was also the runner-up to the Pittsburgh Penguins' Mario Lemieux for the league's most valuable player award.

"We were brought up to feel like a family. [Coach Glen Sather] did a good job of making us feel like a family, making us understand you were only as good as the guy sitting next to you," said Fuhr. "We knew we had a good hockey team, we just didn't realize how good."

His goals-against average dipped below 3.00 just four times during his 19 seasons; he registered only 25 shutouts and closed out his career with a save percentage of .887. In his rookie season, he was undefeated in 23 consecutive games and playing behind the highest-scoring team in the NHL; Fuhr even got involved, registering 14 points in 1983–84—the single-season league record for a goaltender.

His 3.38 GAA, meanwhile, is the highest in the Hockey Hall of Fame and will inevitably remain so. Georges Vezina, inducted in 1945, is next at 3.28, followed by Billy Smith at 3.17. Alex Connell, a 1958 inductee, is the lowest at 1.91.

"I had room to make a few more mistakes than most goalies did, because we scored a lot," Fuhr once said, "but I also had the opportunity to watch probably one of the best teams ever from the best seat in the house."

When several of the players got back together again to play the Montreal Canadiens alumni in the 2003 Heritage Classic, Fuhr was back in net, and at his acrobatic best, splitting the game with Bill Ranford and Andy Moog, in a 2–0 Edmonton win. "That's why Grant's in the Hockey Hall of Fame," defenseman Paul Coffey said. "I don't think there was a better…goaltender in the league or in the history of the game [than] Grant Fuhr."

Born in Spruce Grove, a city that sits 28 kilometers west of Edmonton, Fuhr was a 1981 draft pick of the Oilers. Only one other goaltender, John Davidson, has been selected in the first round.

"I don't think he ever got enough recognition from other people when he was on the Oiler teams," Gretzky once said. " He was happy if we won 8–7 or 2–1. He didn't care about shutouts. He cared about winning, and he was the right guy with the right mind-set to play goal for us."

Fuhr's 40 wins during the 1987–88 season was a team record that stood for 29 years—right up until Cam Talbot moved past the Hall of Famer. Talbot won 42 of the 73 games he played in 2016–17—backstopping the Oilers to their first playoff appearance in 11 years.

29 The Grate One

It was best described as Tikkanese—this curious, inimitable fusion of English and Finnish, intermixed with a little Swedish, that often spewed from the lips of Esa Tikkanen. Even Oilers teammate Jari Kurri, a fellow Finn, was uncertain as to what it was Tikkanen was jabbering about.

Freelance NHL writer Jouni Nieminen? He too is at loss for the words. Nor did he think there was anyone from Finland capable of translating. "Esa is a wonderful guy, but his language is his own," said Nieminen. "Very unique."

"Esa talks twice as much as anybody else," former teammate Craig MacTavish once said. "That's because you can understand just half of what he says."

One of the game's great agitators, Tikkanen has taken up residence on the Stanley Cup often. Drafted by the Oilers in 1983, the feisty Finn didn't join the team until the fourth round of the 1985 playoffs. He went from the world championships to the Oilers series against the Philadelphia Flyers, earning a ring before he'd even played a regular-season game.

Traded to the Rangers in exchange for Doug Weight on March 17, 1993, Tikkanen ultimately registered 630 points in 877 regular-season games, with his most productive spurts spent when he was on a line with Wayne Gretzky and Kurri. When he finally conceded his knees just weren't what they used to be, he returned to Jokerit, Finland, retiring in the spring of 2001.

Upon his retirement, Tikkanen had played in 186 playoff games in the NHL, netting 72 goals—including 11 game winners—and 132 points. And he had five Stanley Cups, four from his days with the Oilers and another with the New York Rangers.

Esa Tikkanen (right) was as flamboyant on the ice as off.

"Always a colorful character on the ice, always a crowd favorite," said Nieminen. "I remember him playing against Canada in the 1985 U20 Worlds in Helsinki. First shift, he levels Claude Lemieux. The Canadians were a little bit surprised—and he just kept talking to them.

"The most important thing about Esa as an agitator, on top of being a great player, a money player with five Stanley Cups and some huge playoff series, is that he did it with such cool style. He might give someone a poke, or push another opponent over the boards into the bench, and he'd drive people nuts asking if they had a sister or something, but he never hurt anyone. Never played dirty, never hit anyone with a headshot like the agitators in the NHL do now," Nieminen continued. "I wrote a long story about Esa when he turned 50, and asked a lot of people here about him, and no one can remember him ever hurting anyone. One of the most colorful players to play in the NHL. A winner."

In 2005 Tikkanen was a player-coach with the South Korean team, Anyang Halla, in a startup league in Asia. According to the report from the 5–3 loss to their Japanese opponent, Tikkanen assisted on Halla's first goal but spent much of the game directing his teammates on the ice…in Tikkanese.

30 Troubled Times

If the 1980s were all about mullets, boom boxes, and Stanley Cups, the 1990s were about Beanie Babies, bleached hair, and troubled times. The value of the Canadian dollar had plummeted, attendance was dropping, and Oilers owner Peter Pocklington was threatening to move the team out of Edmonton if he didn't get a bigger portion of revenue from the Coliseum—and he wanted it renovated.

There were season-ticket drives and the Stay Oilers Stay campaign; beer companies were donating one dollar from the sale of each case sold, and kids were emptying their piggy banks. The Jets had already left Winnipeg, Quebec City had lost their team, and it looked as if Edmonton may quite possibly soon be without NHL hockey—in spite of the team's past successes. It was the dawn of the NHL's new big-money era, and Pocklington was walking a financial tightrope.

The team that had been so dominant was being dismantled bit by bit, piece by piece, and by 1993, for the first time in franchise history, the Oilers missed the playoffs—and would do so for the next three years.

The NHL set up a Canadian Assistance Plan to help offset the US-Canadian exchange rate, but there were conditions that had to be met before the Oilers could qualify for the subsidy. They had to reach a season-ticket target of 13,000, up from 6,800, in addition to selling luxury boxes and board advertising. The Friends of the Oilers, a group of prominent businesspeople assembled by Cal Nichols, went to work and sold enough season tickets to get the base up to 13,482 by the deadline, but there were still troubles ahead.

On June 5, 1997, Pocklington, who owed the Alberta Treasury Branches more than $100 million, announced he was selling the team for $85 million US. "These money problems have taken a lot of the fun out of the business for me," Pocklington said. "Pro hockey is now a place for big corporations with very deep pockets or a group of very wealthy investors."

Les Alexander, the owner of the NBA's Houston Rockets, dropped an $82.5 million US cash offer on the table, which did not include assurances that the team would stay in Edmonton, triggering a location agreement that was written into Pocklington's reworked lease.

Local investors had 30 days to come up with $70 million US—and again, Nichols and his group went to work. On May 5, 1998, the team was sold to the Edmonton Investors Group, an assemblage of 38 benevolent businesspeople and corporations.

"Those years were tough," said Bob McCammon, an assistant coach with the Oilers from 1995 to 1998. "[General manager Glen Sather] was always stick-handling around, trying to make trades. You couldn't keep players."

The Edmonton Investors Group had their struggles too. Season-ticket sales needed to be ratcheted up again in order to get a share of the league's Canadian Assistance Plan monies; a $10 million cash call was required to offset the revenue shortfall.

By 2001–02 the team was operating on a budget of $49.8 million Canadian in a league that had been defined by the haves and the have-nots, which is why the EIG was banking on a salary cap when the collective-bargaining agreement expired in 2004. "We rode the wave for three or four years, in a tough time, with the Canadian dollar being where it was, and there was no salary cap," said Doug Weight, an Oiler from 1993 to 2001. "It was a big challenge for our hockey club, and that was the thing I was most proud of, that we were able to win a couple of series and make the playoffs. In my last six years here, we were sometimes playing teams that were paying $30 to $50 million more than our team was making."

It took the cancelation of the 2004–05 season for the league and the NHL Players Association to come to an agreement. The Canadian dollar was soaring, which was significant given that all the salaries are paid in US dollars.

There were just too many businessmen used to running their own businesses, which brought about some discord within the EIG, and after repeated offers from drugstore billionaire Daryl Katz, the group finally sold him the team for $200 million.

The Two Sides of Ownership

A brash entrepreneur to the core, Peter Pocklington was 14 when he traded his bike and $100 to purchase his first car, which he then flipped for $500. By 1980 he owned a car dealership in Edmonton, a meatpacking plant, a trust company, real estate, and the Edmonton Drillers of the North American Soccer League—and of course the Oilers, which he bought into in 1976.

He signed Wayne Gretzky to a 21-year personal services contract, added the Edmonton Trappers of the Pacific Coast League to his stable, raced jet boats in the same circle as actor Paul Newman, and was friends with former US president Gerald Ford. He was living large.

What he couldn't do was escape the economic downturn in the mid-1980s. Mortgage rates were a staggering 21 percent, unemployment rates skyrocketed, and when his businesses started to spiral downward, Pocklington started using the Oilers as collateral.

He dealt Wayne Gretzky to the Los Angeles Kings in a deal with a $15 million return. It was payment for his line of credit with the Alberta Treasury Branches. "It got ridiculous," Pocklington told the *Journal*'s Curtis Stock in 2013. "They wanted 19 percent a year on the overdraft, whereas now it's 3 percent, and back then, the standard was around 10, 11, or 12 percent a year. The ATB was putting me into a corner. I didn't need the money for my other business. It was money for the ATB."

In 1997 he put the team up for sale, setting in motion a yearlong drama that ended with the Edmonton Investors Group pooling $70 million to purchase the team. For 10 years the EIG were the committed keepers of the franchise—a decade that included the 2006 playoff run. A year later, drugstore billionaire Daryl Katz made a $145 million pitch to purchase the team, an offer that was rejected, as were his next two, the last of which included an additional pledge of $100 million for a new arena.

Several months later he upped his proposal and the group started to soften. Katz purchased the team in 2008 for $200 million, and was soon engulfed in a long, often acrimonious negotiation with the city of Edmonton to have an arena built downtown. Rogers Place, a highly acclaimed project worth more than $600 million, opened in the fall of 2016.

"The previous ownership group did a great job saving the team but nobody was really up for the next challenge," Katz told Sportsnet's

John Shannon. "I can't say I would have been interested in buying the team without the challenge of building a new arena and, through the arena, redeveloping and bringing life into downtown Edmonton... there isn't a sports and entertainment district in the world like [the] Ice District."

The publicity-shy Katz was born into an entrepreneurial family in Edmonton, and didn't stray from his roots. At 29, with his background in corporate and franchise law, he secured the provincial franchise rights to Yogen Früz, the frozen yogurt chain.

He bought the Canadian rights to the Medicine Shoppe in 1991, then added the Rexall chain and expanded into the US. By 2016 the Katz Group had sold its 470 Rexall pharmacies to US healthcare giant McKesson, shifting its focus to its real estate, sports, and entertainment businesses.

The connection to the Oilers wound back through the decades. Early in the Oilers' Stanley Cup years, Daryl Katz was dating Pocklington's daughter, and was soon part of the players' circle. He was from a wealthy family, he was their age, and he established ties that lasted through the years.

After the Heritage Classic outdoor game in 2003, players from the Oilers and Montreal Canadiens attended a party hosted by Katz, who brought in Colin James to entertain the group. When Mark Messier's number was retired, he hosted another bash, this time bringing in the Tragically Hip. In 2003 the Katz Group purchased the naming rights to the Oilers' home rink.

"When he does events like [the post-event parties], you don't see him. He's not like a guy who stands at the microphone and says, 'Look what I've done here.' You wouldn't even know he was there," businessman Lyle Best told the *Edmonton Journal* in 2012.

Katz and his wife, Renee, have been quiet benefactors in the community too, but it is the downtown rink and the surrounding district that has been his public undertaking. "He's got a vision, he's a big-picture guy. He's got a vision of seeing that Stanley Cup presented to the Oilers in a new building downtown," Craig MacTavish, the senior vice president of hockey operations once told the *Journal*'s John MacKinnon. "He's normally pretty good at seeing those visions through."

31 Ted Green Has a Terrible Assignment

It was Ted Green's determination, his grit, that landed him a job on Glen Sather's coaching staff in 1981. The former defenseman was as tough as they came, but not even Green could overcome the Oilers' downturn of the 1990s.

Elevated to the head coaching job in 1991, in place of John Muckler, who had moved on to the Buffalo Sabres, Green was in charge of a team that was in flux. By the time the 1992–93 season rolled around, there were even more roster changes, leaving Green with the onerous task of trying to keep the team competitive. For the first time in franchise history, the Oilers missed the playoffs (and would again in 1994, 1995, and 1996, although Green didn't make it past the 1993–94 campaign).

After the team got off to a 3–18–3 start, including an 11-game losing streak, Glen Sather replaced Green on the bench for the remainder of the season. Green was devastated, but he returned as an assistant in 1997, eventually joining the exodus of coaches who followed Sather to the New York Rangers in 2000.

"I came in under some trying circumstances. There was a revolving-door atmosphere here," said Green, who was also beset with kidney stone attacks in his final season at the helm. "Glen was in a position where he had to make a lot of changes, and I got caught in the middle of that.

"Sometimes during my second and third year of coaching, I was wondering what I was doing or why I was there, but obviously I enjoy[ed] the atmosphere and the environment. I've never lost the desire to be involved with the game at that level."

"Each day was a year for him," Doug Weight recalled in a conversation with Dan Barnes of the *Journal*. "No one bled Oiler blue like Teddy. He felt it so bad. He'd bring it to the rink every day. But we just didn't have the personnel. It was hard, man."

"Terrible" Ted Green, as he was known in his playing days with the Boston Bruins, was involved in one of the worst stick-swinging incidents in hockey. During an exhibition game against St. Louis in 1969, the Bruins defenseman and the Blues' Wayne Maki started swinging their sticks like baseball bats, clubbing each other in the head. Green fell to the ice, his left side paralyzed, the right side of his skull fractured. He was administered last rites before he underwent emergency brain surgery. But he not only rallied after another two operations, he played for the Bruins in their Stanley Cup run in 1972. Both Green and Maki were brought up on criminal charges, and both were acquitted. Maki, tragically, was diagnosed with brain cancer in 1972. He was 29. "Did I think I'd be a head coach in the NHL after Maki hit me? No, I was just trying to add two and two," Green said in 1991. "When something like that happens, you don't think of the future. You think of surviving."

Between coaching assignments with the Oilers, Green had a kneecap removed—decades after doctors at the Mayo Clinic recommended it come out. Green dismissed the recommendation. He wasn't finished playing. It wasn't until 1979 that he called it a career. "They said I had the knee of a 70-year-old. I wonder how old it is today," he said to the *Edmonton Journal*'s Jim Matheson. "I don't know how many operations I've had on my body. I'm not keeping a scorecard. OK, this is 13. It's easy enough to trace all the [surgery] lines on my body."

It was that grit that appealed to Sather when he hired Green as an assistant coach in 1981. "He was a guy who fought back from a very serious injury, a guy who had to teach himself to write with his right instead of his left hand," said Sather. "He had to rehabilitate himself; he's almost a scratch golfer again. When a guy with that determination and spunk is available, you go for him. You don't learn those things out of a book."

32 Swiss Billionaire Story Full of Holes

The city was mired in another of the Oilers' public fund-raising campaigns when Michael Largue, a self-described investment banker from Uniondale, Long Island, strolled into town proclaiming he was not only interested in buying the team but keeping it in Edmonton. He talked his way into a tour of the arena, dined with Mayor Bill Smith, stayed at the Hotel Macdonald, and even collected a few autographed sticks before announcing a deal was a certainty.

He boasted he had the backing of a Swiss businessman by the name of Lester Mittendorf, who had $100 million to spend on an NHL franchise. What he didn't have was Mittendorf's phone number, or anything to back up his claims about his past. The backstory he offered during his outlandish appearance in Edmonton was that he had attended Northeastern University on a hockey scholarship then later played for the Bern Bears in Switzerland, a team owned by Mittendorf. He claimed he had an undergraduate degree from Northeastern as well as a master's degree from St. John's University in Queens, New York.

But the story of Largue and his Swiss backer was full of holes. Reporters at both the Edmonton papers discovered he did not have degrees from either of the schools, nor was there a record of his playing for the Bears. The only Lester Mittendorf reporters could track down was a retired banker in Illinois—and he did not know anyone by the name of Largue.

When the *Edmonton Sun* asked for a photo of Largue, they received a picture of the con man in a shirt and tie, sitting at a tiny kitchen table that was covered in a plastic St. Patrick's Day tablecloth in what looked to be a wood-paneled basement suite.

"The only thing missing was the hot plate," wrote *Sun* columnist Terry Jones.

Largue was actually living with his parents in Long Island but had obviously mastered the science of swindling. His father-in-law called him a loser when reached by the *Edmonton Journal*, and his ex-wife said he was a "pathological liar." It also wasn't the first time Largue had pitched his story to the NHL. He had attempted to negotiate a deal to purchase the Hartford Whalers in 1994.

Capping the absurdity of the saga was that Largue had been convicted of fraud and required permission from his parole offer to travel to Edmonton. In 2007 Largue pled guilty to grand larceny and conspiracy in a sex-extortion scheme in exchange for a prison sentence of up to eight years.

33 The Comeback Kids

There wasn't much to celebrate in Edmonton in the mid-1990s. The team's future was in limbo; the stars of yesterday were long gone. Even the Stanley Cup team from 1990 had been dismantled. By 1994 there were just two players left: Kelly Buchberger and Bill Ranford. But after four straight seasons without a playoff appearance, the Oilers, sparked by the offense of Doug Weight and Ryan Smyth and the goaltending of Curtis Joseph, snagged a ticket to the 1997 postseason.

The first-round series opened in Dallas against a big-budget, star-studded Stars lineup that featured the likes of Derian Hatcher, Guy Carbonneau, Mike Modano, and Joe Nieuwendyk. Dallas took the first game 5–3 then fell 4–0 before the teams reconvened in Edmonton for Game 3—a game for the ages.

Smyth was instrumental in getting the Oilers out of their postseason slump.

It was the first playoff game in Edmonton in five years, but there was little else to cheer about. With the Oilers trailing 3–0 and the third period winding down, more and more fans were filing out of the building. Then the comeback kids started to push back, scoring an "Are you kidding me?" tally of three goals in 1:56. Fans turned back, returning to their seats in time to see Kelly Buchberger score in overtime to give the Oilers a 4–3 win and a 2–1 lead in the series.

The dogged Oilers pushed the series to a seventh and deciding game in Dallas, where the teams again faced off in overtime. Joseph was outstanding. He denied Darryl Sydor on a wraparound, then made a magnificent diving save that prevented Nieuwendyk from ending the series, setting the stage for Todd Marchant, who accelerated past floundering defenseman Grant Ledyard and beat goaltender Andy Moog with the game winner.

"I remember being on the bench, and we were exhausted," said Marchant. "That building was hot, we had played a tough series against an older, veteran team, then Cujo made that save.

"We had the faceoff in our zone and [head coach] Ron Low said, 'Todd, you and Dougie get out there….' We got possession, and I just took off. Dougie put it right on my tape, and fortunately for us, Grant Ledyard fell down.

"That part of it is a little bit of a blur, only because everything happened so fast. What I won't forget is the feeling of elation within the team and the amount of effort and hard work and sacrifice it took to beat a team like Dallas.

"We went into that series not really having a chance. We were just a bunch of young kids," continued Marchant, who scored three other goals during those 1997 playoffs—all shorthanded, which has him tied with Derek Sanderson, Lorne Henning, Bill Barber, Wayne Presley, and Wayne Gretzky in the record books for most shorthanded goals in one playoff year. "I remember our game plan going into that series was to just try and wear them down. Our goal was to get a hundred hits every game. And every step along the way, we just gained more confidence."

The Oilers couldn't get past the Colorado Avalanche in the semifinals series—a series that was over in five games—but they had found a way to negate some of the darker days of the decade. "Everything was doom and gloom about the franchise," said Morley Scott, the team's radio color analyst in 1997. "There was a big black cloud over everything; then Todd Marchant changed it all.

"One of my favorite stories was Game 7 in Dallas. They scored to win it, then the team went straight to Denver for the series against Colorado, so we really had no idea what the interest level really was back home. The Internet wasn't available, Twitter didn't exist, we were talking on hotel phones, not cell phones. But there we were in line at customs when we got back to the airport after Game 2 and we could hear this rumbling sound. All of a sudden it dawned on me that there was a crowd out there to meet the team.

"That goal by Todd Marchant really reversed the fortunes of the organization. That's when hockey became relevant again in Edmonton."

34 Seeing Stars

Time and again, the Oilers would find themselves in the heart of Dallas in the postseason. It was a rite of spring that began in 1997 and continued until 2003. If the Oilers of old had the Battle of Alberta, these Oilers had the Texas Titans.

"Don't get me wrong, playing against Calgary was always a tough game and a battle, but our group had never played them in the playoffs. To this day, Edmonton hasn't played them again," said Todd Marchant. "We played Dallas five years in a row. How does that happen?"

In 1997, 1999, 2000, and 2001 the Oilers and Stars met in the opening round with the Oilers overcoming the odds in 1997 to advance to the semis. In 1998 they eliminated the Colorado Avalanche in seven games, only to fall to Dallas in round two. There would be no playoffs for Edmonton in 2002, but a year later they were back in the playoffs—facing off against Dallas in the opening round.

The Stars had one of the league's highest payrolls; an old, uncomfortable home in Reunion Arena; and, more often than not, the upper hand on the scoreboard. The Oilers were at the Reunion Hyatt so often that waitress Bobbie Zirkelbach knew the players by name and what they wanted for breakfast.

"You can't be so elated one day and so disappointed the next, you can't just physically beat each other up and not hate each other," Oilers captain Doug Weight said after a 4–3 Game 5 overtime loss in 2001. Four of the six games that spring went to overtime, with Dallas winning the series 4–2. "That's probably a strong word," Weight continued, "but it's on the ice, and in the sense of competitiveness, there's no other word that fits."

When the team moved from Reunion to the new but sterile American Airlines Center for the 2001–02 season, the results didn't change for the Oilers, who were eliminated in the first round in 2003.

"People still talk about the Dallas-Edmonton series," said Marchant. "They were battles. For a fan, they were exceptional to watch because it was just good, hard-branded hockey in the play-offs, when everything mattered. Unfortunately we came up short a lot of times, but we were a team that never quit. We got knocked down, we got back up. We got knocked down, we got back up. That was our inexperience, our youth. We weren't going to give up.

"We were an AHL team compared to their team, really. We had a good goalie in Cujo, and we had some good players up front, but you go down that roster to this day, you'd say 'Who?' No disrespect to any of the players, but we were just a bunch of kids called up from the minors or guys who had potential but hadn't really made a name for themselves as everyday NHL players."

That acrimony, at least, was something both sides agreed on. "Nowadays you would have 10 suspensions," Stars coach Ken Hitchcock told Postmedia. "We were laughing about it—there were a couple of games where at the end of the night there were 150 fights. The way it is [officiated] now, the power plays would be 5-for-10. They were very emotional contests. We ended up winning a lot of close games, but more because we had a bigger budget than Edmonton did at the time. But man, they were really good series."

The rough-and-tough battles of attrition that took center stage every spring couldn't have started at a better time for Edmonton. Crowds had declined to the point where season-ticket drives became a common lament in Edmonton. Salaries in the NHL were rising, the Canadian dollar was dropping; there were threats that the team could move, and then it was put up for sale. Then the 1997 Oilers found a way to rally back from a 3–0 deficit in Game 5 and Marchant found the back of the net in an overtime win in Game 7, energizing the team's weary supporters.

"We went through a tough period where all the good veteran players were being traded away for younger players," said Marchant. "I was part of it. I got traded from the New York Rangers for Craig MacTavish, and it took until 1997 for us to finally get back into the playoffs. The feeling around the city was unbelievable because [fans] felt like the team was finally back to where it had always been. It was a huge turning point for the organization."

35 Just Win, Baby

When the wins started to pile up, when the six-game win streak stretched to seven, the clock was turned back to 1985. Rookie center Mike Comrie was 4 years old then; goaltender Tommy Salo was 14. An era had ended, legends had retired, and one team record was about to fall.

With captain Doug Weight leading the way, the 2000–01 Oilers revised an entry in the team record book, winning nine straight games from February 20 to March 13. The previous mark was eight, set by the 1984–85 Oilers, who won eight straight games between January 19 and February 3, 1985, on the way to their second Stanley Cup. "To be a part of history with the names that brought five Stanley Cups to this organization is a great honor," said Shawn Horcoff, a rookie in 2000–01. He was six years old in 1985.

"This is pretty special," said Weight. Everybody in here will remember this."

The shadow that the Stanley Cup Oilers cast is a long one, one that won't be erased. But many of the teams that have followed have wanted to create their own identity. That has been no easy task.

The 2001 Oilers were even on the cusp of missing the playoffs, were it not for the nine-game win streak. It began with a 5–0 win over the Los Angeles Kings on February 20 and continued with wins over the Calgary Flames, Dallas Stars (in overtime), St. Louis Blues, Minnesota Wild, Toronto Maple Leafs, Buffalo Sabres, Carolina Hurricanes, and Tampa Bay Lightning (also in overtime).

"Sixteen years ago we won eight in a row. I can barely remember back that far. I know I didn't have a stomach back then. I sure do now," Dave Hunter told the *Journal*. "But this year's team? I really like what I see."

During the nine-game run, the Oilers scored 35 goals and allowed 13. Salo played 192 minutes and 53 seconds without allowing a goal, moving him past Curtis Joseph into the top spot as the holder of the record for the longest shutout sequence.

But after elbowing aside the ghosts of Oilers past to set the record, the Oilers couldn't get past the Florida Panthers, settling for a 2–2 tie and a 10-game unbeaten streak, which was the backdrop for a raucous home game against the defending champs, the New Jersey Devils. It was the team's first game on home ice since it set the record, and just to add more sizzle to the event, the Devils had arrived for that March 17 contest with a nine-game win streak of their own. It was only the seventh time in the NHL that two teams with streaks that long had squared off, and the first time since the 1979–80 season. In front of the 10th sellout of the season, the Devils won 6–5 in overtime, extending their win streak to 10 games.

The Oilers closed out their final 10 games with a record of 4–4–2—collecting a total of 93 points, which got them a matchup with the Dallas Stars in the Western Conference quarterfinals. They lost the series 4–2.

Their win streak is still in the team record book. "You want to make sure you leave your mark on the city...you want to do something really special," Weight said before the team set off for their playoff meeting with the Stars. "That's why that record was so special. It was something that meant a lot to us, as a team, to beat the team of the '80s."

36 The Year of the Underdogs

It was Game 81, and the Oilers had the Anaheim Ducks across the ice and a tenuous hold on the eighth and final playoff spot in the Western Conference. They took care of the first order of business with an Ales Hemsky goal in the dying seconds that lifted Edmonton to a 2–1 victory over the Ducks. Then the Oilers players and coaches waited…and watched the scoreboard, waiting for a result from San Jose, where the Sharks were playing the ninth-place Vancouver Canucks. So began the Oilers' improbable, intoxicating 2006 playoff run.

The Oilers closed out the regular season with a record of 41–48–13—their first 40-win season since 1987–88—but all it did was earn the underdogs an opening-round showdown with the mighty Detroit Red Wings, who had claimed the Presidents' Trophy with a commanding 124 points. "If anything, this season has been about illogical conclusions," head coach Craig MacTavish said after the Oilers had secured their playoff berth.

Ditto for the postseason, which first galvanized the city then captured the attention of the country. "The '06 run was a chance for a whole new fan base, a whole new group of Oiler fans, to have their time and to be proud of their team and not listen to their parents or grandparents talk about the '80s," said Kevin Lowe, then the general manager of the club. "I run into kids now, and some of them don't even know who Wayne Gretzky is, and that's not a bad thing. It just means life moves on."

The Oilers frustrated the Red Wings with a defensive scheme that pushed them to a stunning series win. It took six games—two that went to overtime—but it was only the start. Edmonton went on to take down the fifth-seeded San Jose Sharks and then beat the

Anaheim Ducks in five games, in spite of a flu bug that ravaged the Oilers dressing room during the Western Conference Finals.

It was the first conference finals win for the franchise in 14 years, and it earned the Oilers the distinction of becoming the first eighth-place seed ever to make a trip to the Stanley Cup Finals. They were the first team to convert a penalty shot and to rally back on a shorthanded goal in overtime. And they had rallied from a 3–1 series deficit against the Hurricanes to take it to seven games.

"When you're in the moment, you get so caught up [with] staying focused on the situation…. You don't want to get side-tracked," said Fernando Pisani, who solidified his place in postseason folklore, leading the league in playoff scoring. "It's later, when you sit back, that you say, 'Wow, that was a bit surreal in the way that it all came together and the way that we played.' We beat Detroit in the first round. Who would have thought we'd even take it to five games?"

An audible gasp could be heard around the country when goaltender Dwayne Roloson left the opening game against the Hurricanes with a knee injury to end his time in the net—and he had been effective for the Oilers since a March trade with the Minnesota Wild. But the Oilers continued to push forward, and eight weeks after the playoffs began, they posted a commanding 4–0 win over the Carolina Hurricanes to take the series to a winner-take-all Game 7 in Raleigh on June 19.

Pisani scored another game winner in Game 6, in front of a euphoric crowd in Edmonton, goalie Jussi Markkanen registered a 16-save shutout, and it appeared the Oilers had the upper hand in the series. "There were two times in that series I thought the Oilers were going to win it," said Morley Scott, then the color analyst for the team's radio broadcasts. "That's when they had the lead early in Game 1, before Roloson got hurt, and after Game 6. That might have been the best game I ever saw the Oilers play.

"Honestly, we all knew it was a magical run that couldn't be duplicated, but it's hard to believe that Game 7 in 2006 was the last time they'd play another playoff game for more than a decade."

The 2005–06 season had dawned with revamped rules, most notably a clampdown on hooking and interference, and a new collective-bargaining agreement built around a salary cap that was to level the playing field for the smaller-market teams. The new CBA had cost the league the 2004–05 season because of a long, drawn-out labor dispute between the NHL and its players, but the Oilers were able to land superstar defenseman Chris Pronger, a former Norris Trophy winner, when the St. Louis Blues needed salary room.

Veteran center Mike Peca was also acquired from the New York Islanders that off-season; then when help was needed on the blueline in January, Lowe picked up Jaroslav Spacek and Dick Tarnstrom. Winger Sergei Samsonov was a deadline deal Lowe swung, as was Roloson, who was the pièce de résistance. "Roly was at the top of his game," said Shawn Horcoff. "And he's probably, to this day, the best big-game goalie I've ever really been around. You just knew."

"[I'm] still pretty sore every time I go to Carolina," said Roloson. "I get pissed off walking into that building."

37 Roloson Saves the Day

When 36-year-old journeyman Dwayne Roloson arrived via a deadline-day deal with the Minnesota Wild, even his new general manager admitted his win-loss ratio was a little unnerving. But what Kevin Lowe saw in Roloson was a fix for their issues in net after auditioning Ty Conklin, Jussi Markkanen, and Mike Morrison. "He's got the good pedigree. He played in the All-Star Game, won the goals-against award. Just a solid, solid, competent goaltender," Lowe said after trading a first-round draft pick as well as conditional selection to the Wild to secure Roloson. In other words, Lowe was willing to overlook the fact that Roloson had played 269 regular-season games over eight seasons, that he'd just once even played 50 games in a season, and that he'd lost more than he'd won over the course of his career.

Unadorned by a wealth of dazzling statistics, Roloson proceeded to play 19 straight games for the Oilers and put up good enough numbers to help push the team into the playoffs. By the time June rolled around, the Oilers had knocked off the Detroit Red Wings, San Jose Sharks, and Anaheim Ducks to advance to the Stanley Cup Finals, and Roloson was 12–5–0–1 when the team arrived in Raleigh, North Carolina, to take on the Carolina Hurricanes.

"You talk about leadership," said defenseman Steve Staios. "When he came in, it helped us build confidence to get to this place. He has made us all better players."

"It's just night after night he gives us that great goaltending," Ethan Moreau added. "All we need is a chance, and he gives it to us."

That's why there was an audible gasp when Roloson crawled out from under Hurricanes forward Andrew Ladd and teammate Marc-Andre Bergeron in the opening game. He was left with a hyperextended elbow and a damaged right knee ligament that didn't require surgery but would require time to heal. His playoffs were done.

The Oilers managed to push the series to seven games before it all came to an unsatisfactory end, leaving many to wonder what the result would have been if Roloson hadn't been hurt. There wouldn't be a reprise either. What immediately followed the 2006 playoffs was an exodus of players—most notably defenseman Chris Pronger. The team failed to get back to the playoffs, and Roloson's game reviews were often varied. At one point he even lost his starting job to Mathieu Garon, but he did rebound, as the unflappable goaltender had done in the past.

In 2008–09 Roloson set up shop in the Oilers' net and played 36 consecutive games, even turning in a 51-save performance near the end of the run. When the Oilers were officially punted out of the playoff race, Roloson turned the net over to Jeff Deslauriers. He left the team that summer, leaving a one-year, $3 million contract on the table in favor of a two-year, $5 million deal with the New York Islanders. The Oilers responded by signing Nikolai Khabibulin to a four-year contract worth $3.75 million per season—another of the club's signings that just didn't pay off.

Roloson, who was creeping up on 40 years of age when he left and signed with the Islanders, was nowhere near the finish line. In the 2010–11 playoffs, after having been traded to the Tampa Bay Lightning in January 2011, he was in net for the Lightning, registering a record of 10–6–0–1 before the Bolts bowed out to the Boston Bruins in the seventh game of the Eastern Conference Finals. He went into the record book as the oldest goaltender to register a playoff shutout when the Bolts beat the Pittsburgh Penguins 1–0 in Game 7 of the opening round. He was 41 at the time. Roloson played one more season, then hung up his mask.

38 The Stars Were Bright, Fernando

During Fernando Pisani's fabled playoff run, Todd Harvey good-naturedly feigned surprise when his exalted teammate made it to practice after netting two third-period goals in a playoff series–clinching game against the Detroit Red Wings. "I thought they would have still been carrying him around on their shoulders through Castle Downs," said Harvey. Such was Pisani's world during the Oilers' magical playoff run in 2006.

He was the hometown hero, the revered winger who scored 14 goals in 24 playoff games. Five of his goals were game winners, not the least of which was a memorable shorthanded overtime goal in the fifth game of the Cup Finals against the Carolina Hurricanes. "I was getting phone calls from guys I went to school with and from people I had never heard of," said Pisani, now a development coach with the Edmonton Oil Kings. "They were coming out of the woodwork, but it was fun. Everyone was excited, especially here in Edmonton."

The third child of Maria and Cosimo, Pisani learned to skate in the neighborhood of Castle Downs in the city's north side. He was an Oilers fan growing up, a player who took the blue-collar route to NHL. Selected in the eighth round of the 1996 draft, Pisani spent four years cultivating his game at Providence College, followed by two-plus years in the American Hockey League. When he finally got into his first regular-season NHL game—as a pinch hitter in January 2003—he was 26 years old. He scored a career-high 18 goals through 80 regular-seasons games in the 2005–06 season—not exactly the kind of production that would have warranted much attention going into the playoffs.

Fernando Pisani (34) scores the game-winning goal in overtime against Carolina Hurricanes goalie Cam Ward during Game 5 of the 2006 Stanley Cup Finals.

He was the unlikeliest of heroes who was at the center of many a conversation in Little Italy, a neighborhood tucked into an area north of the downtown core. "Sure, there's an interest, because its hockey, but with Pisani, well, we know the guy. We know his family. It's closer to our hearts," said Gino Marghella, the deli manager at the Italian Center Shop. "We're big fans of Fern because he's a local kid, and he's shown that perseverance will get you somewhere." And on it went in a community where even debates about the upcoming World Cup of soccer took a backseat to discussions about Pisani.

Playing alongside Michael Peca and Raffi Torres in the postseason, he opened the playoffs with five goals against the Detroit Red Wings—one more than Peter Forsberg scored for the Philadelphia Flyers that spring, and two more than Joe Sakic scored for the Colorado Avalanche in their postseason opening round. Not one player had a better shooting percentage than the unassuming winger who had just 11 shots on net in the series against Detroit. "I'm sure Fernando occasionally wakes up in the middle of the night and high-fives himself. I would if I was having that type of playoff," Oilers coach Craig MacTavish said.

And he was not a one-series showstopper. Pisani kept scoring against the San Jose Sharks, the Mighty Ducks of Anaheim, and the Carolina Hurricanes in the Finals. Timely goals. Game-winning goals.

With the shorthanded Oilers on the brink of elimination in Game 5 of the Cup Finals, Pisani's overtime goal sent the series back to Edmonton. It was the first shorthanded overtime goal ever scored in a Stanley Cup Finals.

"There's always one line that does more than is expected, and that's how teams go deep," Pisani said. "All three of us just caught fire and it seemed like everything I was shooting was going in the net so I was just making sure I got everything to the net."

Pisani was never able to recapture that magic, and he had his issues with injuries and illness, but even if his career didn't end the way he wanted, he secured his place in playoff lore. "It was a great feeling to be a part of that hype that was around the city, especially being from Edmonton. To say that I actually did it in my hometown and that I was able to help create that energy and excitement for everybody in the city was pretty special to be a part of."

39 Murray's Return Engagement

Rem Murray knew all too well that tomorrow wasn't guaranteed, that the game could end at any time. It certainly appeared his career was over before he was able to find his way back to the Oilers, just in time to play a role in their 2006 playoff run. That's why every shift mattered to the veteran that spring. Every period. Every game. "I certainly never expected to get to this point a year and a half ago. Given where I was and where I am now, I feel very fortunate," Murray said of his journey, which began when he was playing with the Nashville Predators.

Suffering with the onset of cervical dystonia, a debilitating disease characterized by involuntary muscle contractions of the neck, Murray first noticed a change in 2003, when his head started shaking after games. He tried to dismiss the symptoms, but the tremors started occurring more frequently and his head had started to pull to the left. He didn't want to worry his wife, who was then pregnant, and he did not want to jeopardize his playing time, so Murray tried to push through it, through the pain, until he couldn't hide it any longer.

He was diagnosed quickly, and what followed was a cycle of muscle relaxants, Botox treatments, and a rigorous physical therapy program. After struggling with day-to-day challenges such as the simple act of pouring milk into a cereal bowl, Murray, who had spent six seasons with the Oilers at the start of his career, finally started to find some relief, and eventually he made it back onto the ice.

After a tryout with the Detroit Red Wings, he secured a spot with the Houston Aeros in the American Hockey League. Then the Oilers, looking to add some two-way depth to their lineup, called. Murray got into nine league games that March and another eight in the playoffs. Every shift mattered. Every game was a bonus. "I certainly take everything in that I can, especially when I go out and warm up before the game," he said during the playoff run. "I take that atmosphere in more than I would have. Earlier in my career, it's not that I took it for granted, but I was just out there playing the game. I'm doing that now too, but I certainly enjoy every aspect of it now."

Murray played another six years—all in Europe—before hanging up his skates in 2012.

40 Pronger's Early Exit

When the Oilers' riveting Stanley Cup run came to its abrupt end, so too did the team's time with its preeminent defenseman. Chris Pronger, who had signed a five-year, $31.25 million contract 11 months earlier, had asked for a trade at the insistence of his wife, Lauren, who just couldn't get comfortable with the idea of living in Edmonton.

Patrick LaForge, then the president of the club, said the management group assessed their options but in the end followed through on his request. What he didn't know then was the kind of impact Pronger's departure would have, that it would be the start of another free-fall for the franchise. Even Pronger's teammates would have been hard-pressed to predict how big a void he was going to leave.

"Let's not kid ourselves—he was one of the best defensemen in the league at the time," said Fernando Pisani, who led the scorers in the 2006 playoff run. "Any time you lose a piece like that, you're going to have a hole. He was playing over 30 minutes a game and was controlling our blueline, our back end. That's a big void to fill.

"We were always a team that would pride ourselves on working hard and being in games, always fighting for that last playoff spot, but when you bring in a guy like Pronger…he just added another element to our team that we never had before…. We knew it was going to have an impact; we just didn't know how much."

There were a number of other players who bolted town as well, which did not help the Oilers—on the ice or off. Jaroslav Spacek (Buffalo), Georges Laraque (Phoenix), Michael Peca (Toronto), Sergei Samsonov (Montreal), Dick Tarnstrom (Switzerland), Rem Murray (Finland), and Radek Dvorak (St. Louis) all departed before the 2006–07 season.

But Pronger was a difference maker. He was an intimidating presence who could take away time and space. He could control a game. As the Philadelphia Flyers' Scott Hartnell once told *Sports Illustrated*, "Chris was the best player in the NHL at knowing where you didn't have padding."

"Intimidation was his long suit for sure," said LaForge. "He could do things no player I had seen could do when it came to controlling the game. That Bobby Orr kind of guy who decided what pace we were going to play at. And he was a guy who demanded a level of commitment to success in our locker room, and on the bus, and on the plane, and at dinner. He was relentless in that regard. I watched him in the locker room tune guys up after a game.... When you take that pillar out, it weakens the building. But I didn't have any idea [about the impact it would have].

"There wasn't an opportunity to get full value for what he represented. It didn't happen anyway. I don't think anybody is to blame for that. It was just such a short timeline to get done."

LaForge said there were discussions amongst the management group about their options, including the rot-in-hell tactic, that it would be their call as to when—or if—they would trade him. "That was definitely part of the conversation but is that the way you treat a player of that status? He almost delivered us a Stanley Cup," LaForge continued. "Anyways, everything was contemplated, but the right thing to do was to try and make a value-for-value deal—and we know how that turned out."

A few short weeks after Game 7 in Raleigh, North Carolina, the Oilers traded Pronger to the Anaheim Ducks, taking back young sniper Joffrey Lupul, defensive prospect Ladislav Smid, and three draft picks.

Lupul, 23 at the time and under pressure to offset Pronger's departure in his hometown, just couldn't find his game in Edmonton and was eventually traded to the Philadelphia Flyers. Pronger too ended up with the Flyers after three seasons with Anaheim—including the Ducks' 2007 championship season. His career certainly didn't end on his terms. A serious eye injury, which was followed a few weeks later by a head injury, left him coping with post-concussion syndrome.

He was inducted into the Hockey Hall of Fame in 2015, and after the announcement of his induction, he said in a conference call that it had been a tremendous ride in Edmonton with a team that really believed it could win it all.

The Oilers, meanwhile, ended up creating a family liaison role a few years later. It was part of the team's plan to be more proactive in the way that they transitioned players and their families, particularly with so many big-name free agents spurning contract offers. "The team changed significantly after that [playoff] year," said Pisani, "but Pronger was a blue-chip player. He just elevated everybody's game."

41 No Thanks, I'll Wait for Stanley

It's been decades since the Oilers held up the Stanley Cup in celebration, but they did uphold tradition the last time they got close. When the Oilers laid claim to Clarence Campbell's chalice in 2006, team captain Jason Smith avoided making contact with the trophy after their Western Conference victory, subscribing to the theory that the Stanley Cup is the only prize worth celebrating.

Some in hockey's traditional circles have even suggested it would be in poor form to touch a trophy when there is a much bigger prize still up for grabs. Those with superstitious natures believe that to handle the memento would only jinx the team's fortunes in the Cup Finals. So many a captain has refused to lay a hand on the silverware.

In 2006 Smith shook the hand of deputy commissioner Bill Daley after the Oilers defeated the Mighty Ducks of Anaheim, posed for a picture with the Clarence S. Campbell Bowl, then skated away without touching the trophy. Georges Laraque even went so far as to cover it up with a towel while it sat in the visitors' locker room at the Honda Center.

"Jason didn't grab it and skate around with it, so it set the tone," said Fernando Pisani, who led the Oilers with 14 goals in the 24 playoff games that spring. "I don't think anybody ever said anything about touching it or going near it. As a player you just kind of know, 'Okay, that's great, that's one part of our goal, but the big one is the Stanley Cup. That's the one you want to end up holding and skating around with.' It was great that we had gotten that far, but everybody's focus was, 'All right, let's get ready for the next game.'"

Talk of the tradition surfaced again in 2016 when Pittsburgh Penguins captain Sidney Crosby, obviously willing to buck years of folklore, held the Prince of Wales trophy after the Pens had defeated the Tampa Bay Lightning in the Eastern Conference Finals. It wasn't the first time, either. There was much ado in 2009 after Crosby touched the trophy after the Penguins defeated the Carolina Hurricanes to win the conference. They went on to win the Cup Finals, defeating the Detroit Red Wings 4–3. A year earlier, Crosby had stuck to tradition, avoiding contact with the trophy, and the Penguins lost to those same Wings. The Penguins beat the San Jose Sharks to win it all in 2016.

"Although we haven't accomplished exactly what we want, we still accomplished something here," Crosby said in 2009. "You know, we can still enjoy it."

"I think we overthink everything," added center Jordan Staal. "It's a great thing to win this trophy."

In 1991 captain Mario Lemieux not only touched the Wales Trophy but actually skated around in celebration with it. The Penguins won their first Stanley Cup in team history in the following round against the Minnesota North Stars. The Philadelphia Flyers' Mike Richards held up the trophy in 2010.

The Oilers of old were certainly regulars in the conference finals, but in spite of their youth, they were staunch traditionalists. They did not touch the trophy then either. "There was a lot of stuff that the Oilers did that may have come from other teams or from other players, but that was just part of the mentorship," said former equipment room manager Barrie Stafford. "We had a lot of traditional ways. It was just an unwritten rule that we hadn't won anything. Just leave that trophy alone. On to the next step. I don't even remember anyone talking about it. You just didn't touch it." It was obviously a tradition Mark Messier did not take to the New York Rangers. He held up the trophy in 1994.

As for the Stanley Cup? Tradition has it that it does not get touched unless you've earned the right by playing for a winning team.

42 With Glowing Hearts

By day, Paul Lorieau was a dispenser of glasses and contact lenses. He was an optician with an alter ego, because on those nights when the Oilers were playing at Rexall Place, Lorieau was the sharp-dressed tenor singing the Canadian and American national anthems. Lorieau also made the singing of "O Canada" a heart-warming, can't-miss event during the 2006 playoffs.

By the time the teams were in Edmonton for Game 3 of the Western Conference Finals, exuberance had hit a crescendo. The underdog Oilers had knocked off the Detroit Red Wings, dispatched the San Jose Sharks, and were now sparring with the Anaheim Ducks for the right to advance to the Stanley Cup. And Lorieau had a plan.

Days before Game 3, President Patrick LaForge and Stew MacDonald, the executive vice president of marketing and sales, were kicking around ways to transform the Oilers, the last of the country's playoff contenders, into Canada's team. Playing on patriotism—after San Jose fans had booed the Canadian anthem—they went to Lorieau with their idea for a sing-along. Lorieau started as he had so many times before, then raised a hand encouraging the fans to join in, before holding his microphone high up in the air, allowing the fans to take over.

Not only did the plan work to perfection—Lorieau was ready to pull down the mic to resume singing if it didn't—it became a signature gesture that carried on through the rest of the playoffs. And it solidified Lorieau's stature.

"It was pretty inspiring," head coach Craig MacTavish said the day after. "I've never seen that before...credit to Paul Lorieau to have the sense to let it happen. One of those unforgettable moments in a Stanley Cup run."

Born in the Alberta town of Legal, Lorieau's passion was opera, and it once took him to New York for an audition with the Metropolitan and New York City Opera companies. When he returned to Edmonton, his sister informed him that the Oilers were looking for a new anthem singer. Lorieau dropped off a demo tape and the rest, as they say, is history. For three decades, he sang the anthems in Edmonton, earning the kind of stature afforded the likes of Roger Doucet in Montreal, Wayne Messmer in Chicago, and Karen Newman in Detroit.

His voice was quieted too soon. Lorieau, who once described the anthem as "a nation's prayer," passed away from esophageal cancer on July 2, 2013. He was 71. Just two years earlier, surrounded by his 4 daughters, 5 grandchildren, and 13 extended family members, all wearing No. 30 Lorieau jerseys, he sang his last anthem at Rexall. The Oilers presented him with a commemorative print and a trip to the Metropolitan Opera in New York to mark his retirement. That night, he turned the microphone over to the crowd one last time—a gesture that was not forgotten.

Before the Oilers played their last game at Rexall Place, a video of Lorieau holding up his microphone played on the big screen. A choir of 16,839 joined in, setting the tone for the building's sentimental send-off.

When the club finally returned to the playoffs in the spring of 2017, Robert Clark, like Lorieau, gained recognition across the country for turning the microphone over to the enthusiastic crowd of 18,000. "I've done opera productions, I've done all sorts of things in front of thousands of people, but nothing compared to how I was feeling that first game," Clark said in one of the many interviews that followed. "How could you not be pumped being a part of something like that? It was just insane."

Prior to Game 1 of the opening series against the San Jose Sharks, Clark was in the stands singing the first few lines of the anthem before turning it over to the fans, a practice he carried on through the playoffs. "It's certainly a good homage to Paul Lorieau. At the same time, it's original and it's about now. It's something that has never been done before. That's what makes it great."

43 Big Money Trumps Small Market

Doug Weight was a 22-year-old second-line center making $205,000 when he first stepped into the Oilers lineup. Acquired from the New York Rangers in exchange for Esa Tikkanen in 1993—a time when Edmonton's veterans were being offloaded for younger, more affordable options—Weight found his way. He developed into one of the NHL's top centers and accordingly made his teammates better.

With the exception of the year he missed 34 games with a torn medial collateral knee ligament, he was the team's s top point producer, registering 104-, 82-, 70-, 72-, and 90-point seasons while playing a tough, smart, defensive game. He took over the leadership of the team and assumed the role of consummate star with ease.

But Weight was now 30 and due a raise on his $4.3 million contract. He was a restricted free agent who was going to be unrestricted in 2002, which was going to put him out of the Oilers' financial range, at least until a new collective-bargaining agreement was in place.

He also had arbitration rights, and Oilers general manager Kevin Lowe could not, would not, run the risk of having a third party set the salary, so he dealt his center to the St. Louis Blues for Marty Reasoner, Jan Horacek, and Jochen Hecht.

Losing star players had become an all-too-familiar scenario for Oilers fans. Wayne Gretzky was traded to the Los Angeles Kings in 1988. Mark Messier, Paul Coffey, and Glenn Anderson were among those who had been dealt back in the day. Bill Guerin, more recently, was traded to the Boston Bruins when the Oilers decided he was too expensive to keep.

Then it was Weight who was moved. The small-market Oilers were out of their league when it came to playing with the big-budget, free-spending franchises such as the Colorado Avalanche. The Avs were able to spend $50.5 million for Joe Sakic with enough left to pay goaltender Patrick Roy and Rob Blake. And the Blues, who lost Pierre Turgeon to the Dallas Stars for $32.5 million that July, had the money to spend on Weight, who pocketed a five-year, $40 million contract.

"It's a shame it had to come to an end like this with a trade," said Weight. "But there is a bit of inevitability to it…I just signed a great contract—a no-trade deal. We can go buy a house, a beautiful place to live, and the first reaction from my wife and I was tears. It's hard to explain how close a team it is. That's what I told a lot of the guys, for a team like Edmonton, with a small budget, they need more camaraderie, more heart, to be competitive.

"I wanted to be back, but they couldn't offer me more than $6 million. That's obviously a huge amount of money, but they made the decision. Now I go on.

"Nine years is a third of my life, but I couldn't pick a better scenario. I'm going to an organization that has consistently been committed to winning."

44 What Prompted Todd McFarlane to Buy In?

When the Oilers' future was hanging precariously in the balance, and Cal Nichols was feverishly searching for ownership partners, comic book artist Todd McFarlane anted up. It was worth the experience, he acknowledged.

The Spawn creator was one of the 38 members of the Edmonton Investors Group that purchased the Oilers in 1988, effectively blocking the transfer of the team to Houston business-man Les Alexander, who likely would have moved the team to Texas had his offer been accepted. Ten years later, Daryl Katz bought the team, and McFarlane returned to life as a casual geeky fan creating his comic chaos from his home in Phoenix.

"Yeah, it was cool to be part of it," McFarlane said of his con-nection to the team, "but the downside of it was that I was the only guy on the ownership team who wasn't local. So I didn't get to go to all of the home games or training camps and practices. I wish I had been closer to it...but when they played in Phoenix, I got a chance to go golfing with some of the guys, which was cool."

McFarlane was definitely hands-on with the design of the team's first alternate jersey, which was blue, white, and silver with a bold new logo. "Industrially modern" was McFarlane's vision. Soon after Katz bought the team, the jerseys were mothballed and a retro version was introduced.

Born in Calgary, with ties to Edmonton's Londonderry area, McFarlane was an Oilers fan during the team's glory days. He was a sports aficionado, and baseball was going to be his avenue to the pros. The sport got him a scholarship to Eastern Washington State University, but after his dream of playing professional ball was derailed by an ankle injury, McFarlane turned his attention to comic books.

In his mid-twenties he was an illustrator at Marvel, and before long, he became recognized as one of the most celebrated cartoonists in the business. He eventually launched Image Comics, whose signature hero is Spawn.

Expansion into music videos, electronic games, television, and feature films followed, as did a line of sports figures and action figures for glam rockers KISS. NHL figures too fell into the McFarlane Toys inventory. One of his prized projects was building a Wayne Gretzky figure. "One time when I met [Gretzky], I was outside his house, 3-D scanning him for a toy, and when we were done, he invited me in, made me lunch, and served it to me! I was like, 'Wow!'" said the man who once paid $3 million for Mark McGwire's 70th home run ball. "Here's a person who chose a profession and exceeded better than anyone," McFarlane continued, "yet he came across as a guy who was so humble about it. You don't run into a lot of celebrities who know they're the best and don't read their own headlines.... He's a huge inspiration and example for the youth, and that's why I like him. I don't really buckle my knees with celebrities, but he's the only guy I've ever met where I felt like a 10-year-old boy."

These days, McFarlane says he's just an Oilers fan who catches the occasional live game when the team is in Phoenix to play the Coyotes. And yes, he still has the third jersey he helped create… more than one. Sometimes he even gives them away as gifts.

"I don't follow them as closely as I did. When you are involved, you're in the thick of it. But now I'm back to being a casual, geeky fan. I'll always have a soft spot for the Oilers."

45 And with the Sixth Pick, the Edmonton Oilers Select...

When Edmonton played host to the 1995 NHL Entry Draft, the *Edmonton Journal* hired a lip reader in an attempt to tap into some of the draft floor conversations. Very little was gleaned from that exercise, but no one had to guess what the crowd was thinking when the Oilers selected Steve Kelly with the sixth pick, rather than Alberta-born Shane Doan.

The 1995 draft had been destined for Winnipeg but needed to be relocated when it looked like the Jets were about to close up shop. Edmonton had 2,500 hotel rooms available for July 7–9, and the Coliseum had air-conditioning, which became a requirement after people had passed out in the Colisée de Quebec two years earlier, and in seven short weeks, everything was in place for the sold-out marquee event.

The Oilers went in with the sixth pick overall, a selection determined by the league's first draft lottery, and as general manager Glen Sather and chief scout Barry Fraser made their way to the podium, a chant of "Doan! Doan! Doan!" began. The big right-winger from the Kamloops Blazers was clearly the people's choice...but Steve Kelly was the Oilers' selection.

"Hey, I liked Doan a lot when we interviewed him," Sather said that day, acknowledging he had heard the chants. "I know this is a homegrown kid, a farm kid, with a great personality and a lot of fans here. I liked him on an emotional level, but emotions don't make that choice. Too many people in our organization had seen both of them play, and I questioned all the scouts at our table, and every one there said this guy [Kelly] is the better player.... I guess we'll just have to wait two or three years to find out who was right." Kelly played 149 NHL games, 27 with Edmonton, scoring one goal.

The Jets snapped up Doan with the seventh pick, and the Halkirk, Alberta, product went on to carve out an exemplary career in the NHL, moving with the Jets to Arizona. He remained with the franchise.

46 An All-Star Moment

The images are grainy, clearly wearing the passage of time, but on January 2, 1979, 17-year-old Wayne Gretzky stood at center ice at the Edmonton Coliseum, flanked by Mark Howe and his 50-year-old father, Gordie, for the start of a WHA All-Star Game against HC Moscow Dynamo.

Gordie Howe had played more All-Star Games than Gretzky had played regular-season games, and for the young star, it was an indelible moment. "I was just happy to be picked to play on the same team with Gordie," he said, "to be on the same line."

Gretzky hadn't thought there was anything that could have topped a promotional tour he was on that past summer with Howe and WHA star Bobby Hull. During the trip to New York, he even had a chance to meet boxer Muhammad Ali in the lobby of their hotel.

"Part of the reason I made the [All-Star] team was because the series was in Edmonton," Gretzky told Postmedia's Jim Matheson years later. "I mean, I was doing okay, but [I was] not a top 20 player in the league. When I went down to the morning skate the first day, I was just excited about being in the team picture. I thought I wouldn't play one shift, and I was fine with that."

Gretzky was sent out with the Howes for the opening faceoff because coach Jacques Demers thought it would settle his nerves. And 35 seconds later he scored the game's first goal, then added another. The trio registered eight points, including the points they picked up on Mark Howe's winner in a 4–2 victory.

"[It was] one of my greatest thrills," said Gretzky, who figured he weighed about 155 pounds at the time, and was swallowed up by the jersey they gave him. "[Howe] grabbed my jersey, got a needle and thread, and sewed the one side to make it smaller. I was thinking, *This is something my mom would do*," said Gretzky. "I've still got that jersey."

When the two were sat on the bench, Gretzky said to Howe, "Boy, I'm really nervous." Howe yawned, stretched, and said to Gretzky, "So am I." Gretzky said later, "He told me just to get the puck to him and he'd get it in, and on our first shift, that's what happened."

There were a mere 8,038 on hand to witness that historic moment, although the crowds grew as the three-game exhibition tournament wore on. There were 15,590 on hand for the final installment, which the All-Stars won 4–3.

Gretzky turned 18 a few weeks later, and to mark the occasion, a cake was wheeled out to center ice at the Coliseum, along with a bottle of champagne and a 21-year contract.

47 Play Ping-Pong Like an Oiler

Want to add a diversion to your hockey routine? Try Ping-Pong. Back in the Oilers' infancy, a table was rolled into their dressing room, and it has remained an integral part of the club's culture. Players compete in matches after a practice, sometimes before games. Even on the road, if they can find a table. During the 1997 playoffs, the players managed to appropriate a hotel meeting room in Denver and spent an off-day playing Ping-Pong. General manager Glen Sather picked up the tab for the $250 table.

In Edmonton, the trainers would use the Ping-Pong table for storage; owner Peter Pocklington once used it to store a bounty. He dropped $100,000 down on the table and told the players that if they won the 1991 Smythe Division Finals against the Los Angeles Kings, the cash was theirs. The Oilers beat L.A. and split the money between the players and the dressing room staff.

"If you go back and look at photos from the '80s, that Ping-Pong table was in the middle of the room," said longtime equipment manager Barrie Stafford. "We put towels on it, and drinks on it, sticks for signing, even sweaters after the game. It was part of the dressing room. And it was used constantly. Those guys played Ping-Pong all the time."

The Oilers are certainly not the only team to have set up a table in their room. Ping-Pong has become such a dressing room pastime in the NHL that veteran Dominic Moore even created an annual off-season fund-raiser called Smashfest. Since the inaugural event in 2012, there have been countless NHLers who have attended. Oilers goaltender Cam Talbot has been a regular; defenseman Darnell Nurse has also taken part, with monies raised going to cancer and concussion research. And whether it is a game at Smashfest

The Oilers' Ping-Pong table has been a familiar sight in the team's locker room for decades.

or a friendly contest in the Oilers dressing room, there are some lightning-quick skills on display.

"They used to have an old wooden [table] that was handmade, and all the players from the past had signed it," Shawn Horcoff said during his captaincy in Edmonton. "They sold it for charity at one point, then we got another one…it was part of the room forever."

When the room at Rexall Place underwent a $3.5 million renovation, the table—and the tradition it represented—disappeared. Horcoff got another table in the room. It went missing again when Dallas Eakins was coaching. He had it removed, much to the dismay of the players. After he was fired, it made its way back into their quarters. But not without some small concession.

Almost immediately after Todd Nelson stepped into the interim head coaching role, several players approached him about getting the Ping-Pong table back. He told them they'd have to earn it, and after they had won their first game under his direction, the table was dusted off and put back into service.

48 Devilish Repartee

Throughout his storied career, Wayne Gretzky was as diplomatic as he was prolific. Except for that one time he happened to express his thoughts about the New Jersey Devils. It was November 19, 1983, and the Oilers had just thumped the Devils 13–4 in front of their Edmonton fans. Gretzky had racked up three goals and five assists—his first eight-point outing in the NHL. Jari Kurri netted the remaining five goals, the majority of which were scored on an embattled Ron Low, Gretzky's former teammate.

Gretzky said later that it was the sight of Low and his backup, Chico Resch, fishing pucks out of the net that sparked his infamous postgame remarks that night. "It got to the point where it wasn't even funny," Gretzky said. "How long has it been for them? Three years? Five? Seven? Probably closer to nine. They struggled in Kansas City, they were awful in Colorado, and now look what is happening.... It's about time they got their act together. They're ruining the whole league. They had better stop running a Mickey Mouse organization and put somebody on the ice."

He sent an apology to the Devils the next day, via a telegram, but owner John McMullen had reached his breaking point. The franchise had already been the subject of parody song titled "Devil's Dance" by Men Without Hat Tricks—a takeoff of the top 40 song

"Safety Dance" by the Canadian group Men Without Hats. "We can lose if we want to" was one of the notable lines in the spoof.

Bill MacMillan was relieved of his coaching duties and replaced by Tommy McVie, who had been coaching the American Hockey League's Maine Mariners. For good measure, McMullen stripped MacMillan of his general manager title.

The Devils won just 17 out of the 80 games they played that 1983–84 season. "It was ridiculous," Resch told NJ.com almost 30 years later. "Ronnie was battling, but the score was getting up there, and in the middle of the second, Billy says, 'You're in there.'

"I was brilliant for the rest of the second. I was really cooking, but the stove got turned off really quick. The third period it started crashing down, and it was overwhelming. I remember we got a power play and they put out Gretzky and Kurri to kill it. I went to the bench and said, 'Guys, we're not scoring nine goals to tie this. Just don't let them score [shorthanded].' Within 30 seconds, two-on-one, in the back of the net."

Because Gretzky's comments were immortalized in headlines on both sides of the border, most notably in the state of New York, there was a welcoming committee of sorts when the teams met again in East Rutherford two months later. Fans were wearing Mickey Mouse ears, the hecklers in the sellout crowd were primed. Sprinkled throughout the stands were a number of signs: MICKEY WHO?, WAYNE, SAY CHEESE, GLEN SATHER PRESENTS: GRETZKY AND THE MOUSEKATETEERS, GRETZKY IS GOOFY.

Edmonton won 5–4 and Gretzky extended his point-scoring streak to 46 consecutive games. "I didn't mean to insult anyone," Gretzky said after the game in the Brendan Byrne Meadowlands Arena. "I'm 23. I made a mistake."

49 Shorthanded, Long Reach

With 894 goals in the record book, a collection Wayne Gretzky racked up in his regular-season outings, and another 122 goals accumulated through his playoff appearances, it is hard to imagine that 1 or 2 particular goals—or 10, for that matter—would stick out. But Gretzky has often pointed to the shorthanded goal he scored against the Calgary Flames in a playoff game in 1988 as his top pick.

It was Game 2 of the Smythe Division Finals—another clash between the provincial foes—and this time around, the Flames were favored to win the series. Calgary had wrapped up their exceptional season with the league's best regular-season record before knocking off the Los Angeles Kings 4–1 in a best-of-five series to advance. The Oilers took down Winnipeg 4–1 in the semis and then had to get by the Flames. "That series was our Stanley Cup," Craig Simpson told Sportsnet years later. "I think our players truly felt if we beat Calgary, we were going to win the Stanley Cup."

The Oilers trailed twice in Game 2, and twice they responded. With four minutes left in regulation, Jari Kurri beat Mike Vernon with a perfectly placed slap shot, sending the teams to overtime. Six minutes in, Mark Messier was sent to the box for tripping Joey Mullen, setting the stage for Gretzky, who hopped over the boards with the penalty killers. He got behind the Flames defense, took an outlet pass from Kurri, rushed up the left wing—tireless in spite of all the minutes he'd played—and teed up a blistering slap shot from a ridiculously tough angle that flew into the far corner to give the Oilers a 5–4 win.

"There was no other place he could have put it," Calgary coach Terry Crisp said. "[But] anytime you blow a 3–1 lead and a 4–3 lead, you have only yourself to blame. Then we get a power play in overtime and they score shorthanded."

The Oilers won the next two games in Edmonton, sweeping the series before going on to celebrate another Stanley Cup win—Gretzky's last.

50 The Battle of Alberta

Theirs was a rivalry so steeped in tradition that when Oilers owner Peter Pocklington was threatening to move the team out of Edmonton, even folks in Calgary were rooting for them to stay. "I overheard someone saying they didn't want the Oilers to leave because they'd have no one left to hate," one Edmontonian said during the team's troubled times.

This provincial conflict, more affectionately known as the Battle of Alberta, dates back decades and transcends hockey. With the proximity of the two cities—one the province's capital, the other the largest in Alberta—it has filtered into the political arena, the business world, and onto the football field. And for a stretch of time, it was one of the fiercest rivalries in the NHL. "Against Edmonton, up there especially," said former Flames defenseman Jamie Macoun, "you had one of three career choices to make: one, get traded; two, quit the game; or three, man up."

The Oilers moved onto the NHL stage in 1979, following the merger of the WHL; the Flames moved to Calgary from Atlanta for the 1980–81 season—and by the mid-1980s, Calgary and Edmonton were the best teams in the Campbell Conference...in the league, really. They would punish each other just for fun. Or just because they could.

The Battle of Alberta rages on as Todd Harvey (right) pins Calgary Flame Eric Nystrom to the boards in 2005.

In a regular-season game in January 1990, the teams combined for more than an hour in penalty minutes. The next season, the teams were at it again, racking up 53 penalties for a combined 227 minutes. "I didn't enjoy it much, and I know our players didn't enjoy it much. It made for some great games, but all in all, I'm happy to be away from it," Wayne Gretzky said after he had been dealt to the Los Angeles Kings.

Between 1983 and 1990, the Oilers were in six Stanley Cups, winning five; the Flames represented the conference in the other two Cup Finals during that eight-year stretch, winning it all in 1989. And five times the teams had to get through each other to advance.

The Battle of Alberta took center stage again in 1991, when the teams collided in the postseason for the fifth time—the final time, as it turned out. And what a series it was, arguably the best opening-round series that spring. It was the Oilers' vast wealth of playoff experience versus the Flames' talent. It was rough and fast-paced. It was Theo Fleury clashing with Jeff Beukeboom, Grant Fuhr in one net and Mike Vernon in the other. And it was renewed confrontations between centers Mark Messier and Joel Otto.

So evenly matched were the teams that it took an overtime goal from the Oilers' Esa Tikkanen in Game 7 to end the Smythe Division semifinals series. "These teams put on a series everyone in North America watched.... The Flames have nothing to be ashamed of," said Adam Graves after the Oilers won 5–4. "Just like we'd have nothing to be ashamed of if they had scored in overtime."

Through the five playoff meetings, the Flames won once, and that was in 1986, when defenseman Steve Smith put the puck into his own net.

The rivalry has been simmering for some time now. The Oilers have only made one playoff appearance since 2006, and while they advanced to the Stanley Cup Finals in 2006 before they were defeated by the Carolina Hurricanes in Game 7, it was their first and only appearance in the Finals since 1990. The Flames were in the Cup Finals in 2004, losing to the Tampa Bay Lightning.

"Well, I guess it's because the competitiveness went out of the rivalry," captain Craig MacTavish said when the financially strapped Oilers had been reduced to a shadow of their dominant selves in the mid-1990s. With so much heated history, and so much anticipation for a renewal, the rivalry will surely flare up again when the teams meet again in the postseason. Only twice since 1991 have both teams even advanced to the playoffs in the same spring.

"So many great players and so many characters," Fleury told Flames writer George Johnson before the doors at Rexall Place closed for good. "We had so many great battles in there. A lot of crazy stuff, yeah, but so much great hockey.

"What the kids today need is another playoff series to rekindle that spark we had in the late '80s and early '90s. Hopefully in the years to come we'll be talking about all the great games the Flames and Oilers have played in that new rink in Edmonton and the one they're looking to build in Calgary. It's up to them to make the memories now."

51 And in This Corner... Muhammad Ali

When the incomparable Muhammad Ali passed away in 2016 at the age of 74, memories flooded back to all those who had been in contact with the boxer. Among those paying tribute to the Greatest was the Great One.

"The very first time I met him was in a locker room in Los Angeles," recalled Wayne Gretzky, who was playing for the Oilers when he first met Ali. "He just came right up to me and said, 'So you're the Great One. Just remember, I'm the Greatest.' It was a pretty nice moment." It was also just one of the moments where Ali and the Oilers crossed paths.

During the summer of 1983, Ali and Dave Semenko took part in a charity boxing match that drew 6,000 fans to Northlands Coliseum—each of whom dropped $40 to watch the three-round encounter between Ali, the heavyweight boxing champ, and Semenko, the NHL's unofficial heavyweight commander. In his autobiography, *Looking Out for Number One*, Semenko said he trained for the fight but didn't look the part, walking into the ring with an old pair of black high-top runners and a crimson-and-silver terrycloth bathrobe.

"We hadn't even thought about it, but I'd been wearing the robe when they laced the gloves on me," wrote Semenko. "So there we were, standing in our corner with the opening bell about to ring and I couldn't get the damned bathrobe off over those great big sixteen-ounce boxing gloves." His cornerman, Rocky Addison, a former Manitoba middleweight champion, whom Semenko met while playing in Brandon, unceremoniously cut off the sleeves with a pair of trainer's scissors.

Semenko opened with a left jab according to reports of the June 12, 1983, fight, but otherwise few punches were traded during the choreographed round. The trademark Ali Shuffle—that mesmerizing back-and-forth shift of the heavyweight's feet—even made an appearance while Ali played to the crowd. In the final minute of the third round, Ali reportedly threw a flurry of punches that caught Semenko off guard, but in the end, the fight was declared a draw.

It was Mark Messier's uncle Larry who orchestrated the boxing event in Edmonton as well as a visit to Ali's California mansion. At the time, he had been working for Ali's entourage, selling promotional mementos. When the team rolled up to the boxer's mansion in Beverly Hills, not all that far from the homes of Mick Jagger and Jane Fonda, they came with gifts. The Oilers presented him with an autographed stick and a cake in the shape of a boxing ring, to commemorate his 41st birthday.

Ever the lyricist, Ali said to the group: "I love your company and I admire your style, but your gift is so cheap, I hope you don't come back for a while."

52 The Royal Wedding

Blissfully unaware that their adopted son would soon be traded to another team, in another country, Edmonton's denizens reveled in the nuptials of Wayne Gretzky and Janet Jones. With the pomp and ceremony reserved for royalty, the couple, both 27 at the time, married on July 16, 1988. Thousands lined the streets outside the St. Joseph Basilica on Jasper Avenue to catch a glimpse of the couple. Nurses at nearby Edmonton General Hospital even tried to switch shifts so they could sneak a peek from the windows.

The national networks carried footage from the wedding, and snippets of the scene were sent stateside, to *Entertainment Tonight*, Robin Leach's *Lifestyles of the Rich and Famous*, and *Good Morning America*. "Nobody takes a day off [here] when the queen is here, or on election day. Or [for] the Wayne Gretzky wedding," said Steve Makris, who was the photo editor at the *Edmonton Journal* at the time.

Jones wore a $35,000 satin dress adorned with rhinestones, pearls, and hand-beaded crystals; the wedding cake had seven tiers and was decorated with fresh flowers and Austrian crystals; and the Edmonton Symphony Orchestra played during the 33-minute church service. There were eight bridesmaids, eight groomsmen, and among the 650 invited guests were musician David Foster, actor Alan Thicke, and Soviet hockey star Vladislav Tretiak.

Both local newspapers printed special sections the next day, and outside the church, onlookers invested in the futures of hot dog and ice cream vendors.

"Everything was big," teammate Dave Semenko recalled years later. "There were more people. More bridesmaids. More everything than any other wedding I've ever seen. It was like a Hollywood premiere."

Gretzky bought Janet a Rolls-Royce Corniche II convertible for a wedding present, team owner Peter Pocklington gave the newlyweds a pair of scooters, and the city of Edmonton's gift was a replica of Alexander Graham Bell's original telephone.

"I hope he and his new wife produce five more Wayne Gretzkys," said Tretiak.

Videographer Don Metz, handpicked by Gretzky to film the event, had a crew of cameramen and three editing suites in the basement of the church for the exclusive production. What he didn't see was what was to come. When Metz was driving the couple

Lasting Impression

Steve Makris, the photo editor at the *Edmonton Journal* in 1988, was stationed outside the church on the day of the wedding, orchestrating his crew. He saw the who's who of hockey come and go, along with the celebrities who were on the guest list, but it was the image of one guest in particular that stuck with him long after the church ceremony.

"I noticed that there was one limo that did not leave. It was parked off to the side—waiting for Gordie Howe," he said. "He stayed until he had signed every autograph for every fan standing across the street from the church.

"He could have just as easily got[ten] into the limo and left for the reception.... I remember it like it happened yesterday."

A Sweet Jab

With the provincial rivalry between the Oilers and the Calgary Flames at its peak in the 1980s, maybe it was only fitting that a Calgary chocolaterie would take the opportunity to get in a little jab.

Gretzky and his bride-to-be ordered chocolate Bernard Callebaut hearts for their 650 dinner guests, but when the chocolates arrived from Calgary, they were in boxes inscribed with the Calgary Flames logo. The hearts were promptly transferred to white boxes that had been engraved with the couple's name and the wedding date.

to the airport a few days after the wedding, he just happened to ask Wayne when he'd be back. The hockey star said, "How does October 5 sound?" Twenty-four days after the wedding, Gretzky was traded to the Los Angeles Kings.

53 Good to Know

Coconut water and lactic acid had not made their way into the vernacular when Wayne Gretzky's wizardry was weaving its way into the NHL's record books. Heck, he'd scarf down a hot dog (or two) an hour before a game—not exactly the kind of cuisine on a sports nutritionist's list.

He was particular about his routines too. He would always dress the same way on game days, finishing with the tuck of his jersey into his hockey pants. Always on the right side. When he headed out on the ice for warm-ups, he'd intentionally miss the first shot wide right, and he was always the second player out on the ice before the opening faceoff.

He didn't like his sticks touching other sticks either, and accordingly, he would often tuck them away in a corner. The stick preparedness went further than that. Gretzky would routinely put baby powder on the blades, in part because it had become part of his superstitious ways, but also because he was convinced that less snow would stick, leaving the puck unaffected.

And with that, here is some more good-to-know miscellany:

- Gretzky's linemates for the eight games he played with the Indianapolis Racers were the towering Kevin Nugent and Angie Moretto. Nugent, 6'5", was a 1975 Boston Bruins draft pick who played 25 games with the Racers then went to work on Wall Street. Moretto, 6'4", also left the game after the team folded that 1978–79 season. After attending the University of Michigan, he played five games with the NHL's Cleveland Barons. Gretzky was back in Indianapolis on September 25, 1987, for an exhibition game between the Oilers and the St. Louis Blues. Just 5,591 fans showed up.

- In 1994 seven ex-Oilers were in the New York Rangers lineup: Mark Messier, Kevin Lowe, Glenn Anderson, Craig MacTavish, Adam Graves, Jeff Beukeboom, and Esa Tikkanen. The Rangers won the Cup that spring.

- At the inaugural home game of the Toronto Road Runners (then the Oilers' farm team), Oilers GM Kevin Lowe was to drive out to center ice at the refurbished Ricoh Coliseum for his introduction. But twice the announcer said, "Ladies and gentlemen, Kevin Lowe," and twice the doors to the truck stayed shut. Turns out the child locks had been activated, and with the building's lights dimmed and the vehicle's windows tinted, no one saw Lowe banging on the window, trying to get out.

- In 1993–94 Gretzky, then with the Los Angeles Kings, topped the leaderboard with 130 points, but he also had the distinction of doing so with the worst plus-minus of a scoring champion (minus-25). Nine years earlier, as an Oiler, he had the league's best plus-minus (plus-98) and won the Art Ross Trophy with 208 points.

- If you need more evidence as to how dominant the Oilers were, there's this statistical note. Jari Kurri scored 71 goals in 1984–85, but it still wasn't enough to net him the scoring title, which went to Wayne Gretzky, his linemate, who finished with 73.

- Nelson Skalbania had not seen Gretzky play before he tied him to a contract with the Indianapolis Racers, so he flew the 17-year-old to his home in Vancouver and tested his stamina by taking him out for a 10-kilometer run.

- The 1983–84 Oilers averaged 5.58 goals per game. That team, as well as the 1985–86 team, included three 50-goal scorers and four 100-point players.

- There is a carrot on all five of Edmonton's Stanley Cup rings, with bites taken out after each championship.

- Edmonton played host to the 40th NHL All-Star Game on February 7, 1989, and in front of a sellout crowd, Gretzky scored one and added two assists. He was named MVP and collected a car for the honor—the 14th car he'd won. He turned the keys over to Dave Semenko.

54 The Ultimate Fan Experience

If the idea of chowing down on a Breakaway Burger in Wayne Gretzky's restaurant in Toronto isn't appetizing enough, or if a bottle of chardonnay from Wayne Gretzky Estates won't suffice, one needs to consider a week at his fantasy camp. Providing, of course, money is no object. This splashy event, which is regularly sold out, takes place in Las Vegas and is as over-the-top as the city itself.

In return for a hefty registration fee of $14,999 US, participants check into the Bellagio hotel, where they are immediately treated to a taste of life in the NHL. Camp-goers are outfitted with practice jerseys, sticks, pants, gloves, and helmets—gear that is fit for a pro. There are professional trainers; coaches such as Cap Raeder, Larry Robinson, and John Muckler; even a pre-tournament draft.

Over the five-day event, one can rub shoulders with NHL alumni such as Jari Kurri, Grant Fuhr, Chris Chelios, Denis Savard, and of course Gretzky himself. Wayne's father, Walter Gretzky, is a regular at the event, and proceeds from the camp are funneled to the Great One's foundation, which helps provide less fortunate kids with hockey equipment and ice time.

"We know now how the event runs, so we know when the guys are going to see Gretz for the first time," said trainer Chris Hamelin. "That's the best part, watching the first-year campers. You see these people who are so successful in life, whether they're CEOs or in upper management or whatever, and then they end up around these guys. They see Gretz for the first time or sit beside him on the bench or, heaven forbid, catch a pass from him, and they're like little kids. They step outside of who they are and into this."

Hamelin has worked seven of the camps, including the 2016 event in March. His first trip was in 2009, and it was his honeymoon. Instead of having a big wedding, Monique Hamelin wanted a smaller affair so she could take part in the camp. Chris Hamelin volunteered to assist the training staff.

"It's gotten big. The year Monique was there, we had three teams, maybe four. Now there's 100 participants and 20 to 25 pros," said Hamelin. "We had six teams [in 2016]."

The first edition of the ultimate camp for weekend warriors was staged in Scottsdale, in 2003, at a cost of $9,999. Paul Coffey, Glenn Anderson, and Bobby Hull were among the stars who joined Gretzky for that event.

An Enhanced Stat on Mr. Corsi

Jim Corsi once relayed a story about how his kids' friends thought it was quite something that their surname was just like the Corsi number, the name of an advanced hockey statistic. Not just *like*, as it turns out.

Jim Corsi, who once played with Wayne Gretzky, is the creator of a statistic that was modified and championed in the analytics movement. It's why he has wryly suggested he's become an inanimate object.

Recognized as one of the league's first full-time goaltending coaches, Corsi spent 16 seasons with the Buffalo Sabres before joining the St. Louis Blues, and along the way, he came up with a mathematical formula to assist his netminders. "Their friends would say to them, 'It's cool, you have the same name.' They'll say, 'Well, no, it's my dad,'" Corsi said in an interview with Eric

Duhatschek of the *Globe and Mail*. "It's quite a funny story how it got that name, but I'm okay with that. I don't feel marginalized. I'm actually quite pleased in the grand scheme of things."

An engineering student in his native Montreal, Corsi credits both Ken and Dave Dryden as two of his mentors. He got his shot

Longtime goaltending coach and analytics pioneer Jim Corsi has revolutionized the way the position is played.

in Edmonton when Dave Dryden retired, and what followed were conversations about the science of coaching goaltenders. Ken convinced him to give hockey a chance after he had secured his degree. Dryden's message to him was that the engineering would always be there; hockey wouldn't.

Corsi, the goaltending adviser, played for the Oilers in their first season in the NHL, winning 8 of his 26 games—the only games he would play in the NHL before he eventually made his way over to Italy to close out his career. "And here I am. No slide rule or calculators," Corsi told the *Edmonton Journal*'s John MacKinnon.

After Corsi retired following the 1991–92 season, he returned to North America and was teaching part-time, consulting when possible, and looking for work in the NHL as a goaltenders coach. He has since worked with Dominik Hasek and Ryan Miller while he was with the Sabres, devising his statistical formula.

Corsi figured the true measure of a goaltender's game couldn't be determined only by shots on net. He concluded that tracking a blocked shot or a missed shot also required effort, so he developed his formula to measure a goalie's workload.

His intent was to help the goaltenders he was tutoring train more efficiently. Instead Corsi, the enhanced stat, has morphed into a formula for measuring the shot-attempt differential of a player on the ice, with an end goal of quantifying puck possession.

"It was not enough for me to say, 'Okay, do a drill.' I was trying to see where our weaknesses were," Corsi, the goaltending advisor, continued. "The Corsi stat was more about me finding out what work our goalies were doing, and should we give him a day off or should we work him harder? How much work should we give the backup? Shots on goal was insufficient to measure that.

"As I often tell people, statistics are like a lamppost for a drunkard. They can either illuminate, or you can use it to lean on. Its value is in trying to illuminate."

56 Canada's Gold Medal Custodians

For 50 years, Edmonton's Waterloo Mercurys were the self-effacing custodians of Canada's Olympic title. Forgotten for so many of those years, they didn't enter an Olympic conversation until 1988, when the Winter Games were staged in Calgary, a 300-kilometer drive away. They were honored again in 1998, when a red wool Mercurys jersey, borrowed from the Hockey Hall of Fame, was hung in Canada's dressing room. In 2002 they were finally inducted into the Canadian Olympic Hall of Fame.

Sponsored by benevolent businessman Jim Christiansen, the Mercurys skated onto the hockey scene in Edmonton in 1947. Many worked for Christiansen at his car dealership—Waterloo Mercury—some were firefighters, others were industrial workers, but they all came together to form a team that would go on to win the Western Intermediate League championship. Asked to represent Canada at the 1950 worlds in London, England, they won all eight games in the 10-day round robin, outscoring the opposition 88–5. They were the first Alberta team to win gold on an international stage.

That dominance was on display again in Oslo when they were chosen to represent Canada at the 1952 Olympics. The Mercurys outscored the opposition 71–14 and compiled a record of 7–0–1 to win the country's sixth hockey gold medal.

The Ottawa Royal Canadian Air Force Flyers won gold in 1948; the Soviet Union, which first competed in the Winter Games in 1956, won seven of the next nine titles, the Americans twice. The Mercurys, meanwhile, became the forgotten team. After a victory parade down Jasper Avenue and a party at the Hotel

MacDonald, they slipped out of the spotlight. Several returned to their jobs at the dealership; many never played hockey again.

Christiansen, who had spent tens of thousands of dollars to bankroll the team, going so far as to make up the difference in lost salaries while the team was in Europe, fell ill during his stay in Oslo, and died in 1953.

Their reign may have ended, but what continued was their stewardship. "We've carried that torch for a long time now. It's getting kind of heavy," said Don Gauf before the changing of the guard in Salt Lake City in 2002. Gauf, then 75, had driven down from Edmonton to take in the Olympics. "It's time someone took it from us."

The torch wasn't passed without some struggles by the 2002 Canadian team. Coached by Pat Quinn and under the direction of executive director Wayne Gretzky, the Canadians opened with a 5–2 loss to Sweden and were criticized for their play in a 3–2 win over Germany.

Gretzky uncharacteristically lashed out after a 3–3 draw with the Czech Republic—no doubt looking to deflect attention away from his team, which responded with a 2–1 win over Finland. They went on to defeat Belarus 7–1 to set up a finals against the US in the E Center in West Valley City, Utah. Canada won 5–2 to take the gold—50 years to the day after the Mercurys were crowned Olympic champions in Oslo.

"Nobody had the amount of pressure this team had coming into the tournament," defenseman Al MacInnis said after the game, referring to the gold-or-bust headlines.

"We desperately needed to win this tournament," said Gretzky.

Canada went on to win gold again in 2010, in Vancouver, British Columbia, as well as in Sochi, Russia, in 2014.

The Waterloo dealership, which opened in 1945, is still in business today. A group of players who had played for the Mercurys in the Olympics bought the dealership after Christiansen died, and while it has undergone changes over the years, there's still a piece of the past on-site: a game-day sweater hangs on one wall, a team jacket on another.

57 Push Worth Its Weight in Gold

The season dawned with just the right amount of brilliance to inject Ryan Smyth into any and all conversations about Canada's Olympic team selection. With 23 points in the first 21 games of the 2001–02 season, it didn't look like anything would keep the winger off the international stage.

So his first thought that November night when he lost his balance and fell against the boards—after playing 195 consecutive games—was that he was going to be okay, that his right ankle was going to be okay. It wasn't. Smyth had sustained a spiral fracture of his lower fibula, an injury that was going to test his perseverance, because if he was going to play for Canada at the 2002 Winter Olympics in Salt Lake City, it was going to be an endeavor. "We had him skating in 12 days," said Ken Lowe, the team's longtime medical trainer. "That was toughness. Not a lot of guys could have done that, but Smytty was like that."

Smyth was back in the Oilers lineup seven weeks after his surgery, and one month after he was hurt, he was named to the Olympic team. "I was hopeful of making the team, and I had a good start, then all of a sudden I get hurt," he said. "I thought my dreams were shattered. But Kenny told me they would do everything possible, to not count myself out."

One of the most decorated Canadians to play internationally, Smyth first slipped into a red-and-white jersey in 1995 and set off to play in the International Ice Hockey Federation World Junior Championship, closing out his time with the national team at the 2012 Spengler Cup. In between, there were eight world championships, the 2004 World Cup, plus the 2002 and 2006 Winter Olympics. He was Captain Canada, wearing the *C* on several occasions and producing regularly: a total of 23 goals and 24 assists in 90 games. "It was an opportunity that only came around [once] every four years," said Smyth. "This was the Olympics. There was a lot at stake for me."

Dr. David Reid knew that if they could get in and operate before the swelling started, the healing process would be accelerated. A plate was screwed in the same night he hit the boards—clamped down with 18 screws to prevent the damaged bone from moving— and a few days later Smyth started his rehab. There were days he had to drag himself off to another round of isometric exercises, and there were countless stationary bike rides at 6:30 AM, but it was the end goal that kept him going. "I'm driven, but I'm not going to say I didn't have moments when I questioned things. I remember trying to put my skate on, thinking there was no way it was going to happen. Then when I got on the ice, it was like it was my first time out there. There were so many things I had to overcome to get that chance to play.

"It was devastating through stretches [of the recovery]. I'd get in there, it would be early in the morning, I'd be grumpy and wondering why we had to do it so early, but there was a purpose to it all. There was a reason to do it."

The 2002 team ended Canada's 50-year Olympic gold drought, defeating the US 5–2, one of several gold medals in Smyth's trophy case.

"No one wanted to win a Stanley Cup for Edmonton more than Smyth," said Hockey Canada's Brad Pascall, the general manager of the 2012 Spengler Cup team. "But whenever he hit an [NHL playoff] dead end, he usually opted to keep playing.

Every year, when we called to invite him to play at the World Championship, there was no question what he was going to say. He is a true competitor."

58 A Lucky Loonie, Eh?

Trent Evans was once a rink rat, a self-professed 15-year-old hockey fan who dashed out of his Edmonton home and secured a part-time job with Northlands. He drove the Zamboni as his career advanced, rolled out the red carpet during the Edmonton Oilers' Stanley Cup victories, even studied cooking through Northern Alberta Institute of Technology's culinary arts program, earning certification as a journeyman chef.

Trent Evans was a lot of things in his past, but never was he a coin collector—at least not until he became synonymous with the loonie—the Lucky Loonie. Evans embedded the Canadian dollar coin at center ice prior to the 2002 Winter Olympic Games in Salt Lake City, intent on transporting luck to the country's hockey teams. Both the men's and women's teams won gold—the women in spite of being saddled with eight straight penalties against the US; the men, for the first time in 50 years. "I had no idea [of the legacy it would leave]," said Evans, now the senior manager of sales at Northlands.

As a member of the rink crew at Northlands, Evans worked alongside Dan Craig, now the NHL's ice expert, and was recruited to work as an ice maker at the Olympic venues. Craig was in charge of the ice in Salt Lake City's E Center in West Valley City and the Peaks Ice Arena in Provo. While making ice at the E Center, Evans realized there was no marker at center ice, so after he had done the necessary measurements, he pulled a dime out of his pocket and placed it on the concrete floor before flooding the surface.

Craig then told him they had used a splotch of yellow paint that was "about the size of a loonie." Evans fished out a coin—a 1987 loonie—put it down, and continued on with his ice making.

Evans was supposed to take it out, once word started circulating that there was a coin in the ice. Instead, he melted out some ice, dropped in a dollop of yellow paint, and left the loonie in place. Only this time he didn't mention it, and another chapter in hockey's history—in Canadiana—took root. "You couldn't see it; it was only that splotch of paint," said Evans.

After the game, Evans dug out the coin and handed it over to Wayne Gretzky, Team Canada's executive director. It has since taken up residence in the Hockey Hall of Fame—in spite of a push from the Salt Lake Organizing Committee to have it shipped across the border.

The tradition has carried on too. At the 2015 Pan American Games in Toronto, for example, Baseball Canada's hitting coach, Stubby Clapp, buried a loonie in the infield before Canada beat the US to win gold. There were several coins stashed at venues in Rio de Janeiro for the 2016 Summer Games, including under the green at the 18th hole of the Olympic course and in the lining at the swimming pool, where a two-dollar coin (a toonie) was hidden. Canada won six swimming medals, the most since the country's athletes claimed 10 at the 1984 Olympics in Los Angeles. (Canada also had lucky Penny Oleksiak, who won four of those six medals.)

Since the 2002 Olympics, the Royal Canadian Mint has been producing a Lucky Loonie prior to the Summer and Winter Games. Evans has a collection. He also has the dime safely tucked away. "It's not only a cool Trent Evans story but a cool family story," said Evans, the father of sons Justin and Jarret. "I participated in a few show-and-tells at their school that year.

"Obviously with Gretzky being involved, it takes it to another level as well, but it had a definite impact on my life, especially with the promotions with the mint.

"It's just cool to be in the Hockey Hall of Fame and for the story to come up and be told and to have others take part in the legend—and not just hockey. Tennis and golf and swimming, all kinds of different sports are involved now. It's pretty cool."

The coin was not only on display at the Hockey Hall of Fame, it was touchable. "There's a wonderful photo of [Gretzky] giving the Lucky Loonie to Phil Pritchard, our curator, in the dressing room," said Peter Jagla, the Hall's vice president of marketing and attractions. "That's been on display too, but we've had lineups of people who wanted to rub the Lucky Loonie for subsequent tournaments in order to bring luck to Canada."

59 Hold Your Tongue!

It was another regular-season tussle between the Oilers and the Flames in the Saddledome when the doggonest thing happened. Fed up with taunting from Harvey the Hound, who had climbed atop the glass behind the Oilers' bench—and perhaps just as fed up with his team's inability to push back from a 4–0 deficit— head coach Craig MacTavish reached up and grabbed hold of the signature red 18-inch tongue dangling from the mouth of Calgary's fluffy mascot. He gave it a yank, which is all it took for the tongue to end up in his hand. MacTavish held it up, showed it to the crowd, then promptly tossed it into the stands. Harvey was later spotted with a long red scarf hanging from his mouth. "My

The Cat's Meow

One of the last teams in the NHL to have a mascot, the Oilers joined the fray when they introduced Hunter the Canadian Lynx in the fall of 2016. Named in honor of the late Bill Hunter, the founding father of the Oilers and the Western Hockey Association, the mascot itself received mixed reviews—mostly because it was hard to make the connection between a lynx and the Oilers.

Yet if one were to peruse the contestants who have taken part in the league-sanctioned Mascot Showdown during the All-Star weekends, there are certainly other odd choices. The Toronto Maple Leafs' mascot is a polar bear named Carlton, and the Dallas Stars are tied to a furry green alien named Victor E. Green. Not even the Minnesota Wild know the heritage of Nordy, while the Vancouver Canucks have Fin, an orca whale, who is not to be confused with the San Jose Sharks' S. J. Sharkie. Calgary's Harvey the Hound, meanwhile, made his debut on February 16, 1984, in a game against the Pittsburgh Penguins. He was the first of the league's mascots.

daughter was a little worried. She wondered if I'd go after Barney," MacTavish said later.

Harvey did make a quick recovery and was back on the job when the Flames returned to action three nights later, but there were so many tongues wagging about the incident that even *The Tonight Show with Jay Leno* reached out to get one or both of the parties on the air. The invitation was declined.

What the Oilers' provincial foes did do was hand out 10,000 red felt rally tongues when Edmonton was back in hostile territory. "You deal with a lot of stuff as a coach, and dealing with Harvey the Hound isn't normally in the job description, nor should it be," MacTavish said. "I just thought it was inappropriate, to put it as subtly as possible, for him to be there taunting us.

"I've had a lot of advice, after the fact, on what I should have done with it. [Oilers general manager Kevin Lowe] said I should have tucked it into the breast pocket of my jacket. [Or] like an ascot.... Obviously the tongue wasn't a tie-down or I'd have pulled him inside our bench."

That January night in 2003, the Oilers players responded with three goals in less than four minutes, but still fell short in a 4–3 decision. "I didn't want to be on all the highlights giving it to Harvey the Hound," MacTavish said. "At the same time, emotions were pretty high. We're down 4–0, and we're being subjected to abuse by the Calgary Flames mascot. Ken King, Craig Button [from the Flames front office] were very apologetic afterward. It was embarrassing to them. It's tough to reel in a rabid dog, I guess."

But that wasn't the end of Harvey's troubles. During a terribly destructive flood in 2013, a report surfaced that his head was floating in the middle of the ravaged Saddledome. Pictures then surfaced of the mascot's head caked in mud. Local mascot makers were quick to state that it was a backup head, that the original costume was safely tucked away.

60 On Frozen Pond... Ahem, on Frozen Ground

NHL commissioner Gary Bettman was once asked about the proliferation of regular-season outdoor games, to which he proclaimed, "For teams and markets that want to host this [event], for fans that want to attend, we can't do enough of them. This is an incomparable event.... This is a fan-oriented, fan-driven event, and that's why we're doing so many games so we can bring it to more fans."

And to think it all started with the Oilers brass, who were kicking around plans for a 25th anniversary celebration. The initial, loosely hatched idea was to commandeer the 2004 NHL All-Star Game from the Minnesota Wild. Instead, president Patrick

LaForge and marketing director Allan Watt left the 2002 All-Star Game in Los Angeles wanting more. Instead, a year later, the NHL's first outdoor regular-season game was staged in Edmonton's Commonwealth Stadium.

"We went to the All-Star Game in Los Angeles and it was, in our opinion, very poor," LaForge told the *Journal* on the eve of the 2016 Heritage Classic in Winnipeg. "It was lots of pink flamingos, fluorescent neon, and as I always say, Mats Sundin doing figure eights at center ice…. It wasn't hockey. And it wasn't what I thought the All-Star Game could have been."

It was on the flight home from California that the idea of an outdoor game took root. There have since been games in the venerable Wrigley Field, Fenway Park, and Yankee Stadium in addition to Dodger Stadium in Los Angeles. On a cold, snowy New Year's Day 2014, 105,491 game-goers settled into Michigan Stadium to watch the Toronto Maple Leafs defeat the Detroit Red Wings 3–2 in a shootout.

Edmonton, meanwhile, finally made its return to a Heritage Classic, 13 years later, on October 23, 2016, in Winnipeg, scoring a 3–0 win over the Jets. It was the 19th outdoor game since the 2003 showcase in Commonwealth Stadium. "Tonight is a night full of memories for both teams. Win or lose, you have something you're going to talk to your kids about, your family. You're going to tell stories," Coach Todd McLellan said after his Oilers defeated the Jets. The game had been delayed until the sun was behind the stadium to better the players' vision, a wait that lasted almost two hours. "These games are important for the fans, for the league, for hockey in general, but they're important for the players too. It's a different night. They look forward to it. We do as well," McLellan added.

The Oilers had just four months to pull together the 2003 game, not the year that franchises have now. And there wasn't a template. This was one team, without the aid of the league, planning an alumni game as well as the NHL's first regular-season outdoor game, on a budget of $3 million.

"It took a long time to get the NHL on-side," Nick Wilson told the *Journal*'s Dan Barnes. "They were worried about bad PR."

"We were willing to go with or without the league's permission, because there's really nothing in the league's rule book that says you have to play indoors," said Kevin Lowe, the Oilers Entertainment Group vice chairman. "The league initially was uncertain about everything, but they realized we had our ducks in a row."

When game day dawned on November 22, 2003, it was snowy and frosty, or as the *Washington Post* trumpeted, it was "weather that would make penguins run for cover." The brittle ice was patched, heat packs were stuffed into skates and gloves, tea and hot chicken broth were available on the bench, and Canadiens goalie Jose Theodore pulled a tuque over his mask, an image that is now synonymous with the game.

Mark Messier and Canadiens legend Guy Lafleur were among those scraping snow off the ice between the two 15-minute periods of the Megastars game; heaters ran nonstop at both benches; and 57,167 bundled-up fans who watched the Oilers and Canadiens alumni in the matinee stuck around for the NHL game, which saw Montreal register a 4–3 victory.

It was minus-18.59 degrees Celsius when the puck dropped for the regular-season game, and colder still with the wind chill. "It was much colder the day before the game," Eric Brewer, then a member of the Oilers' blueline, told the league's website in a flashback to 2003. "We went out [for practice] and the ice was just brittle. It was so cold. We hadn't yet decided what kind of heat gear we would wear.... We thought to ourselves, *Oh, boy. This is going to be a bit of a challenge.*"

"We had it the worst," recalled Theodore, speaking for the goaltenders union. His Edmonton counterpart that day was Ty Conklin. "Players would go on the bench and it was like a five-star resort there. They had heaters and hot packs, whatever they needed. Me and Ty needed to stay in net."

The Heritage Classic is now part of the NHL's brand, as is the Winter Classic, which is the league's trademark for outdoor games in the United States. Given the number of games on the calendar, the mass appeal of the outdoor games has diminished, but they are still showpieces in the local markets. In 2013–14 there were six outdoor games staged across North America. There were half that many games in 2015–16 and four in 2016–17.

In Edmonton, interest was such that the game was sold out months in advance. The lottery that was set up for the last of the 7,000 tickets, elicited 700,000 applications, some from as far away as China and Finland. "It was a real novel idea at the time, and I don't think anyone expected what was going to come of it," Messier said before heading out for the alumni game against the Jets. "You couldn't have picked a better city to try it in than Edmonton. It seems like an obvious idea now, but at the time it seemed a little risky. It's become a huge event for the NHL, a great marketing event for the league to link the past, present, and future."

61 The Stories They Could Tell

Twenty years after the Oilers made their NHL debut, the Boys on the Bus were together again in Edmonton for a reunion celebrating the club's 20th anniversary. (*The Boys on the Bus* was the name of a documentary that followed the Oilers throughout the 1986–87 season.) More than 70 players gathered for a reunion dinner and charity golf event, celebrating not only the team's time in the NHL but also its earlier days in the WHA. Over the course of those two

The Stories They Could Tell…If Only They Could Remember

On a day when players were stuffing hand warmers into their skates and tuques over their masks, one fan at the 2003 Heritage Classic in Edmonton's Commonwealth Stadium made a mad dash onto the field, wearing nothing but a T-shirt and a sock. Sometimes alcohol and fans just don't mix.

The streaker was tackled by stadium security guards before he was cuffed and escorted off the field, all of which proved to be a welcome diversion for more than 57,000 brave souls who had turned their cheek to Mother Nature's chill. When Sgt. Chris Hayden was asked if the culprit should have been charged, he just replied, "Don't you think the poor guy was punished enough?"

Any mention of fans gone wild at a game involving the Oilers has to include Raymond Howarth's ill-advised decision to pour a rum and Coke on Calgary Flames assistant coach Guy Lapointe during a game in Edmonton back in 1997. Lapointe took a swing at the fan, assistant Kevin Constantine threw himself into the mix, and enforcer Sasha Lakovic leapt up from his seat at the end of the bench and scaled the glass partition to get at Howarth.

All three were suspended by the league, the Oilers were hit with a $20,000 fine for failing to have enough security, and the 27-year-old Howarth—a lumber equipment operator—drew a sentence of 30 days in prison, a $1,000 fine, and 90 days of probation after pleading guilty to mischief. Lapointe showed up at practice a few days later with a garbage pail taped to his helmet.

"This incident was televised," Crown Prosecutor Clifton Purvis said after making his decision, which took into account that Howarth had previously been charged with drunk driving, mischief, and assault. "It has given the city of Edmonton a black eye." Or as one Calgary fan quipped a few days later, the brawl had rekindled the Battle of Alberta.

Glen Sather, then the Oilers general manager, said coaches had to remain in control, often in spite of all they tolerated. He didn't always adhere to that theory, however, and ended up in court some 10 years earlier because of a confrontation with a fan in Vancouver. "This guy was yelling at me as we were walking out the tunnel, and he was spitting," Sather recalled in an interview with the *Journal* in the wake of the Lakovic melee. "He had this headset on and it was turned up so loud he couldn't hear me.... I just moved the headset off his ear so he could hear what I was saying." Sather was charged with assault and given a conditional discharge.

days in August 1999, just weeks before Wayne Gretzky's number went into the rafters, memories were rekindled and stories were swapped, such as this one from Cam Connor:

"Wayne got a car every year in his contract, and that first summer he asked me if I would look after it when he went home [to Brantford]," began Connor, the first player the Oilers took in the expansion draft. "I told him I'd park the car, a big Lincoln, in my garage.

"But as soon as the neighbor kids found out I had Wayne's car, every morning at 8:30 the doorbell would ring and my wife would answer it. They would ask if Cam could come out and play. She'd say, 'No, he's sleeping' or whatever. So the kids would then say, 'Well, do you mind if we sit in Wayne's car?' My wife would go out, roll the windows down in the car, and six to eight kids would just sit in there for two to three hours."

Dave Lumley, whose empty-net goal against the New York Islanders sealed the Oilers' first Stanley Cup, said the best memory he had was watching what became of the teammates he had played with. "Mark Messier," he said. "If I had a dollar for every time [coach / general manager Glen Sather] said, 'You screw up one more time, Mess, and you're out of here,' I'd be a millionaire. He ends up being one of the greatest leaders in all of sports. And Wayne Gretzky? I sat beside him for eight years. He ends up being the greatest player who ever played the game. Who would have thunk it?"

62 A Tour of the Town

Sure, there's a list of things one can do in Edmonton, if you are just swinging by the provincial capital for a visit.

The monstrous West Edmonton Mall is certainly on every tourist's list. It spans 48 city blocks, houses an indoor wave pool, a roller coaster, skating rink, and hundreds of shops.

But for the hockey aficionado, a trip to Rogers Place is essential. Even if you don't nab a ticket to a game, there's still enough to see, starting with the a look at the vast exterior of the structure and continuing with a walk under the public pedway where the Hall of Fame resides.

Five replica Stanley Cups are on display as well as a stall from the Oilers' original locker room at Rexall Place. Wayne Gretzky's rookie jersey is hanging there, and there's a collection of record-setting pucks from the 1980s on display.

The iconic Gretzky statue has taken up residence outside the hall; there are public art pieces to view, an adjoining community arena which offers public skating slots, and numerous eateries in the area.

If you're looking for other landmarks that have ties to the Oilers of the past, here are a few to consider:

Teddy's was one of Gretzky's favorite restaurant haunts and is located on the corner of 113th Street and Jasper Avenue, just a two minute walk from the St. Joseph Basilica, where the Great One and Janet Jones were married on July 16, 1988. To mark the occasion of the Royal Wedding, Teddy's owner, Saul Reichert, offered free orange and champagne with any eggs Benedict order. Eggs Benedict was Gretzky's favorite brunch choice.

Along 118th Avenue, sits Coliseum Pizza & Steak, a popular stop for game-goers who wanted to grab a bite before a game at the nearby arena. Players too would frequent the family-run restaurant, and when the Oilers won their first Stanley Cup in 1984, they took it to the pizza palace.

A few blocks east of the restaurant is the Eastglen Inn. In the early 1980s, the Oilers would stay there during training camp.

There's Wayne Gretzky Drive, which runs alongside the arena that was home to the Oilers for 42 years; Mark Messier Trail, which is located along a stretch of St. Albert Trail and one of the routes that will take you to Mark Messier Arena; as well as Grant Fuhr Arena, in his hometown of Spruce Grove.

And if you're flying out of Edmonton, No. 99 Gretzky's Wine & Whisky bar is located in the airport's departures area. Aside from a lineup of beer, wine, and whiskeys on the menu, there's also a nod to Gretzky's Polish ancestry: pierogies and sausages. He claims it's a family recipe passed down from his dad's mother.

If you're looking for something more fulfilling than a Bobby Nick's Burger—the burger that's available at Rogers Place and named after Oilers Entertainment Group CEO Bob Nicholson—head down Highway 2 to the Alberta Sports Hall of Fame.

Located on the north side of Red Deer, it features a gallery dedicated to hockey and those who have contributed to the game on regional, national, and international stages as well as displays dating back to the sport's beginnings.

Among the interactive displays is a shootout net and a "You Call the Play" press box, and of course, there are plenty of sporting artifacts to take in.

If you have more time—and extra gas in your tank—a trip to Calgary is definitely worth considering. There, in Canada Olympic Park, which was the site for ski jumping, bobsleigh, and luge competitions of the 1988 Winter Olympic Games, is Canada's Sports Hall of Fame.

63 The Ties That Bind

Janne Niinimaa had made a promise to Brent Saik long ago that one day, after he'd retired, he'd come back to Edmonton and play in the World's Longest Hockey Game, the monumental fundraising marathon that the Oilers' optometrist has been running since 2003. In 2015 Niinimaa did just that. He flew over from Finland to take part in a game that started on February 6 and ended 10 days later.

Niinimaa has other ties that were cultivated during his playing days in Edmonton, and while it's not uncommon for players to establish friendships in their hockey home, the defenseman was bullish about staying in touch after he was traded. He had left his mark during the six seasons he played with the Oilers. "There's only certain people I remember getting traded. He was one of them," said Ken Lowe, who spent 21 years running the Oilers medical room. "We were in Calgary, and when he left, the players sat there for an hour and talked about Janne-isms: 'Remember the time Janne did this. The time Janne did that.'

"I can remember when Janne broke the tip of his finger and I said to him, 'Okay, ice it all night.' He came in the next morning and he had frostbite. He just said, 'Well, you told me to ice it all night.' That was Janne."

A 1993 draft pick of the Philadelphia Flyers, Niinimaa arrived in Edmonton in a trade for Dan McGillis and left in 2003 in a trade-deadline deal with the New York Islanders for Brad Isbister and Raffi Torres. Leaving was definitely not his choice. He's often said he played 741 games for five teams in the NHL, and it was Edmonton where he was most connected to a team and to a city.

Better Late Than Never?

Jouni Nieminen knows Janne Niinimaa well enough that he had a few stories to share about the defenseman...Janne-isms, if you will:

"Janne is a guy who doesn't believe in getting there too early," Nieminen said of Niinimaa's struggles with time management. "Once, it was snowing and he was driving to the airport in his Jeep. And he was late. There was a wooden gate to the [executive flight center at the Edmonton airport], and Janne was speeding toward it. A guy came out and was waving his hands to let him know the gate was closed."

Niinimaa figured he was going too fast to stop in time to save the gate, so he just elected to drive right through it, scattering pieces of wood into the air. It was caught on video by airport officials, and Niinimaa had to pay for the damages.

"Another time, earlier in his career," Nieminen continued, "he missed a flight to Calgary and took the next one out [it was back when the Oilers were still flying commercial]. When he finally got there, he had to get help in Calgary from the airport officials, who drove him to the connecting gate. He barely made it. And Glen Sather was waiting there, not impressed. Janne just says, 'Don't you know I have an aunt in Calgary?'

"Another good story Janne told us [was about] the time he went hunting with Glen Sather. As they were sitting in a little hut, just the two of them, waiting for birds or whatever they were hunting, Mr. Sather's cell phone started ringing. He's talking trades, even mentioning Janne's teammates. Janne says, 'Mr. Sather, if you have any plans of trading me, remember that I'm sitting here holding a shotgun.'"

Since retiring, Janne Niinimaa has been promoting heavy metal bands in Finland and doing some work as a commentator on game days. And for the record, he does have relatives in Calgary, most notably Veli Niinimaa, his father's cousin, who served as the biathlon chairman for the 1988 Calgary Winter Olympics.

News of his trade to the Islanders hit him hard, and it came down after a pregame skate in Calgary. Niinimaa gathered up his gear in the visitors' locker room in the Saddledome and returned to Edmonton, but instead of taking the time to get himself ready to get to Long Island, he went to the Cross Cancer Hospital. Niinimaa spent the night sitting with Brent and his first wife, Susan, who was battling non-Hodgkins lymphoma. "Janne made a promise to Brent when Susan passed away, a few months after the first game in 2003, that after he was retired, he would play [in the World's Longest Hockey Game]," said Jouni Nieminen, a freelance NHL writer based in Edmonton.

64 Suit Yourself

So maybe you don't possess Connor McDavid's sublime playmaking skills, or the imposing stature of Milan Lucic. That doesn't mean you can't dress like a pro. For more than three decades, Sam Abouhassan has been stitching custom suits for the Oilers, a connection that started with Glen Sather in 1979 and has continued through the years.

And he's easy to find. He set up shop in downtown Edmonton when he opened his business in the 1970s and he hasn't ventured far since. "I've been on 101st St. and 101st Ave., with the same phone number, for 38 years," said Abouhassan, who also teamed up with Kevin Lowe, the vice chair of the Oilers Entertainment Group, in 2000 to establish the Tee Up for Tots golf tournament, which has raised millions for the Stollery Children's Hospital.

Abouhassan had $17 in his pocket when he arrived in Edmonton from Lebanon. He was 19 years old, and he'd left behind a tailoring business, but with his country engulfed in a full-scale civil war, starting over was the more tolerable option. He had an uncle in Edmonton and he had tailoring skills, but because he couldn't speak the language he worked as a jackhammer operator for the City of Edmonton for a year and a half. "I've been a tailor since I was 12 years old," Abouhassan said. "I came in with a trade, and I was very good at it, even then, but I couldn't speak English so I couldn't open a business. And I didn't want to work for anybody else as a tailor."

He eventually opened Downtown Tailors in the basement of the fire-ravaged King Edward Hotel, renting space beside a hair salon, a stamp shop, and a modeling agency. Coming up with the monthly rent of $235 wasn't always easy for the 22-year-old, who was making made-to-measure suits when Oilers coach Glen Sather walked in to have some alterations done. Abouhassan offered to make him a suit.

Introductions to Wayne Gretzky, Lowe, and Mark Messier eventually followed. "Glen Sather said to me one day, 'What's with Downtown Tailors? I don't tell people I'm going to Downtown; I tell them I go to see Sam. You better change the name.'" Abouhassan changed the name of his business, and he never had to worry about the rent again. Now located on the main level of Commerce Place, he is recognized as one of the city's premier clothiers.

Abouhassan dressed Gretzky and his wedding party in 1988. The superstar then put the tailor in charge of suits for the coaching staff of the Canadian men's Olympic hockey team in 2002 as well as the coaches and managers overseeing the World Cup team in 2004. Gretzky was on the phone again in 2006 with another suit order, this one prior to the Winter Olympics in Turin, Italy. "The Edmonton Oilers were the best-dressed team in the league, and they were the best-dressed coaching staff in the league. For many years. And I take some of the credit for that," Abouhassan said.

When the collective-bargaining agreement between the NHL and the NHL Players' Association was drafted in 2005, it included a clause that players were required to wear jackets, ties, and dress pants to all the team's games and while traveling to and from those games—unless directed otherwise by the head coach or general manager.

Some favor Hugo Boss suits, while others, such as the San Jose Sharks' Brent Burns, prefer to make a statement in a custom-made look. He is among the NHL players who order their suits from Giovanni Clothes in Montreal. Domenico Vacca, whose father, Giovanni, founded the shop in 1965, told *Sports Illustrated* in 2016 that he travels to all 30 teams before the NHL season starts.

The number of Oilers who come through Sam Abouhassan's doors these days has decreased compared to the days when he was dressing the entire team. Leon Draisaitl has been a customer. Justin Schultz still orders suits and has them shipped to Pittsburgh. "When I was making their suits in the old days, I was their age. Now I'm 60 and they're 19," said Abouhassan. "I still have a few, and I do a lot of Oilers who are playing elsewhere, but hockey players now are more like a corporation. They have people looking after them more than ever."

65 Sharing the Wealth

One of the richer traditions at home games in Edmonton is the 50/50 raffle, with payouts that regularly top $60,000 for the lucky ticket holder. When the Oilers played their first game of the 2016–17 regular season against the Calgary Flames, the jackpot hit $221,155. The winner that night pocketed $110,577.50. The other half of the monies goes to charity, with minor hockey and ringette teams also benefitting from a tradition that has grown substantially since the introduction of electronic ticketing. The system features a to-the-second running total of the prize pot, which has increased sales.

"We were looking into ways to make money for the foundation we put together in 2001," said Patrick LaForge, president of the franchise for 15 years. The technology is certainly used in other arenas, but the Oilers managed to market it in a way that has resulted in some of the best payouts in Canada. The new system came with new pricing: $5 for one ticket, $10 for three, and $20 for 10, and there is no ceiling. Under the previous system, the pot was capped at $30,000. The money is still split between the lucky ticket holder and the Edmonton Oilers Community Foundation.

Since its inception, the EOCF has contributed more than $2.5 million a year to charities and minor hockey groups in northern Alberta and has a number of fund-raising ventures in addition to the 50/50. From its infancy, the purpose of the foundation was to provide the franchise with an avenue to give back to a community that had been burned by former owner Peter Pocklington. "We had come out of the nastiest periods of time where the owner was not only punting the team around, he had offered it for sale to somebody outside the community," said LaForge. "He was also closing Gainers; he was dealing with all kinds of things.... We needed to enhance the relationship with the community. We needed to win back trust and goodwill, and the outflow of that was the foundation. And it needed to donate money, otherwise it wasn't going to be very valuable."

Increasing the proceeds from the 50/50 went a long way to kick-starting that objective. "We were in Saskatoon for the world juniors [in 2010], where they were test-driving the first example of the electronic ticket," LaForge said. "They were even allowed to buy tickets with Visa cards. The pot shot up to $250,000 so fast that they had to stop sales. We came home and said, 'Okay, this is on our Christmas list. Immediately.'" The machines were rolled out in December 2011.

And if you are wondering if that first jackpot in Rogers Place was the team's biggest, it wasn't. One lucky couple took home $336,995 after the April 12, 2017, playoff game against the San Jose Sharks. That jackpot started with a carryover from a previous game then just continued to balloon. As an aside, that was not the largest 50/50 payout in Edmonton. That distinction goes to a raffle staged at a 2014 Canadian Football League game against the Calgary Stampeders. A whopping $697,068 was spent on tickets that July evening.

66 Yet Another Record

Did you know that Wayne Gretzky's commanding performances have even unfolded outside an arena? At the auction house, for instance, where he broke another record. On August 4, 2016, a mint condition Gretzky rookie trading card sold for the staggering sum of $465,000 US during an auction at the National Sports Collectors Convention in Atlantic City. It was the most ever paid for a hockey card, dwarfing the previous record of $94,162 set in 2011 for a similar 1979 O-Pee-Chee card. Both feature the 18-year-old Gretzky in an Edmonton Oilers jersey with a notation on the back that reads, "Wayne is considered the best prospect to turn professional since Guy Lafleur."

The buyer of the mint card wanted to remain anonymous, but in spite of the money shelled out, it was not the most spent for a sports card. In 2007 Ken Kendrick, the owner of the Arizona

Diamondbacks of Major League Baseball, forked out $2.8 million for a rare Honus Wagner card. Considered the holy grail of cards, the T206 Wagner, circa 1909, features the Pittsburgh Pirates' Hall of Fame shortstop and is particularly valuable because so few were circulated after Wagner demanded the card be pulled from distribution.

The cards were produced by the American Tobacco Company, and legend has it that Wagner didn't like the message it sent to children. Another theory exists that Wagner didn't want anyone else profiting from his likeness, and some have suggested that while he chewed tobacco, he eschewed other tobacco products. No matter the reason, the production of his card was limited, and the Wagner card that Kendrick paid $2.8 million to acquire happens to be the same card that was once owned by Gretzky and Bruce McNall, the former owner of the Los Angeles Kings.

They paid $451,000 for the card in 1991 then sold it a few years later for $500,000. It has continued to increase in value and has been the subject of much controversy. Known as the Gretzky T206 Honus Wagner, speculation swirled that it was too pristine not to have been doctored, and following an FBI investigation, Bill Mastro—the former owner and CEO of a sports memorabilia action house—pled guilty in US district court. He admitted he not only inflated listings with fake bids but also sold altered collectibles. The sports memorabilia executive had purchased the Honus Wagner card in 1985 for $25,000, trimmed the edges, then two years later sold the altered card for $110,000. He was sentenced to 20 months in prison.

67 15 Minutes of Fame

His stay in the NHL was temporary, a one-game stopgap kind of temporary stay. But Kurtis Mucha readily tabled his science studies to spend a game warming the Edmonton Oilers bench. Mucha was playing goal for the University of Alberta Golden Bears when the Oilers called to say they were in need of an interim goaltender for a game against the Ottawa Senators. He backed up Ben Scrivens in the 3–2 win.

"Once its over, the players shuffle out of there and you're back to real life. I was back at school the next day," said Mucha of his emergency goaltending role in March 2014. "Still, it was an unreal experience and something I'll always remember."

Over the years, the team has had to scramble to find pinch hitters willing and able to man one of their nets for a practice session, or to play backup for a game. In 2007 Dwayne Roloson was struck by a sudden bout of the flu prior to a game against the New Jersey Devils, which elevated Mathieu Garon to the role of starter and left the backup slot empty.

Enter Aaron Sorochan, from the Golden Bears. He signed an amateur tryout contract, took the pregame warmup, then settled into his seat on the far end of the bench. "I had to check my watch to make sure it wasn't April Fool's Day," Sorochan said of his reaction to the phone call. "I got the best seat in the house, not only to watch the Oilers but to see one of the best in the game, Martin Brodeur. It was a thrill."

The Oilers twice had to enlist help in the 2009–10 season. The first time, Nikolai Khabibulin's back stiffened up following the morning rehearsal for a game against the Chicago Blackhawks, which led to the recruitment of Torrie Jung, a goalie with the WHL's Edmonton Oil Kings. "I was more excited than nervous," said Jung. "There were more people in the stands for the warmup than we get at a [WHL] game."

Four months later, Devan Dubnyk fell ill before a game against the Vancouver Canucks, and Nathan Deobald, a University of Calgary psychology and drama student, got the call to back up Jeff Deslauriers. The Oilers couldn't fly in a backup from their AHL farm in Springfield in time, and the Golden Bears were on their way to the national championships and Jung was on the West Coast. "Best seat I've ever had for an NHL game," said Deobald, the Dinos' third-string netminder.

When Mucha got the call, the Oilers had just undergone another goaltending shuffle, trading Ilya Bryzgalov to the Minnesota Wild and acquiring Viktor Fasth, in a trade with the Anaheim Ducks. Fasth couldn't make it to Edmonton in time for the game. Enter Mucha, who signed his amateur tryout contract—which has no monetary stipend—and readied himself for what was to come. Seeing his name on the jersey was a rush. So was the sight of his name plate on the locker room stall. He grew up in Edmonton's neighboring hamlet, Sherwood Park, so he'd long been an Oilers supporter.

"For me, one of the cooler parts was experiencing that scene after the team went out to salute the crowd. To see 16,000 people on their feet and to hear how loud it was, was something that not everybody gets to experience," he said after guiding the Edmonton Oil Kings goaltenders through a practice session.

Following his second consecutive CIS national college hockey championship, Mucha hung up his pads to take a job as the Oil Kings' development coach. He'd played five years with the university club, winning the CIS Goalie of the Year Award in 2013. He'd set Western Hockey League records for most career minutes played, tried his hand in the ECHL, even had a tryout with the Oilers in 2009.

It was time to step away, particularly with the opportunity he'd been afforded by the Oil Kings. Plus he'd had that NHL moment back in 2014—he still has the game-day jersey to show for it, along with a few signed sticks that he nabbed from some of his interim teammates.

A year earlier, Mucha had been recruited by the Boston Bruins to fill in for an ailing Tuukka Rask at a practice in Edmonton. "As a Canadian hockey player growing up, your dream is to play in the NHL. I didn't get play," he said, "but seeing the game-day experience is different and it is not something that everybody gets to do.

"A couple of my buddies happened to be at the game and they came down and got pictures, so that was pretty cool."

Fasth didn't make it to town the next day either, so the Oilers brought in Canadian women's Olympic team star Shannon Szabados to assist the team at practice. "Not a bad week and a half," the Edmontonian said after the session. "A gold medal in Sochi and practice with the Oilers...it doesn't get much better. I'm on cloud nine right now."

Szabados was right at home in net, having played with the Grant MacEwan University Griffins and NAIT Ooks men's teams. In 2015 she would become the first woman to post a shutout n a men's pro hockey game, turning away 33 shots while playing for the Columbus Cottonmouths in the Southern Professional Hockey League. "I started firing pucks at her early, and she was saving everything I shot, so then I was actually trying to score on her," Luke Gazdic said after the Oilers practice. "I do think we were trying to at least warm her up a little but, then I realized she was damn good at what she does."

In 1980 Jim Grant, then a business student at NAIT and goaltender for the Ooks, got a late-afternoon phone call from the

Oilers, who needed a goaltender to back up Jim Corsi after Eddie Mio had sprained his ankle. Grant received $100 for watching the Philadelphia Flyers win 5–2 to extend their undefeated streak to 36 games. "I would have worked for free," he said after the game, "but they paid me anyway. My girlfriend got a ticket to the game too. And I got to keep the goal sticks I taped."

68 A Stick-y Situation

Over the decades, Barrie Stafford was the diligent governor of the equipment room, and as such, he saw sticks evolve from being all wood, to aluminum shafts with wood blades, to composite shafts with wood blades, to composite two-piece sticks, and finally to the composite one-piece sticks that exist today. "Not evolution... revolution," he said. "Probably the most significant change in the years I was in the league."

One-piece composite sticks were first introduced by Easton in 1999, with Joe Sakic—the master of the wrist shot—among the first to adopt the Synergy model. Before long, the composite technology had overtaken the stick racks in the NHL.

It didn't come without a cost. In 2007 the lighter, whippier composites were retailing for $250, and they were wreaking havoc with NHL team budgets. They were pricey, and they were not durable. The smallest of nicks or the tiniest of cracks would render the sticks susceptible to breakage. Sticks were vaporizing at such a rapid rate that the NHL even started keeping a tally in a study. Team officials grew more frustrated every time a stick disintegrated during a critical scoring opportunity.

The upside was that the composite sticks were virtually identical, unlike the wood sticks, which were bundled in inconsistent batches and often needed modifications at a workbench. Moreover, players became much better shooters with composite sticks. "Everyone's shot is harder. You see third- and fourth-line guys letting them rip from the top of the right circle," Columbus Blue Jackets goaltender Marc Denis once said.

"You never knew if you were going to get a bad batch of bad wood," Brett Hull told the *Toronto Star*, speaking about the old wood sticks. "They never sent the right pattern. So I'd shave it and rasp it and blowtorch it and curve it and step on it."

When the second generation of composites arrived, there was a notable improvement in their sturdiness. They certainly didn't snap with the regularity of their forefathers. They just weren't any cheaper. Teams were no longer paying $50 for a stick, so stick budgets vaulted into the neighborhood of $450,000.

"The big challenge came with the guys who used them for slap shots," said Stafford. "That's when the revolution took the budgets to a new level.... And I think at one point, they actually had an influence on winning and losing. Very few changes in equipment had that impact. But those sticks, the way they used to break... you'd be on the power play, down a goal, and your d-man would walk in...*boom*, the stick broke. Boom. Another stick broke. It had an effect on the game, never mind the budget. It turned the whole industry upside down. But they also improved the performance of the players. That was a key factor. Guys could shoot better. They could shoot harder."

The last Oiler, the last NHLer, to hold out was Ryan Smyth, who used a composite shaft and a wood blade. "My first year I had used [an all-wood stick]," he said. "I remember [Glen Sather] coming up to me and picking up my stick, twirling it around, and he says, 'You gotta change your curve.' I said, 'Okay,' took it back, and never did change it. He probably still thinks to this day that I did."

69 Hat's Off

Devan Dubnyk had settled into the Oilers net on the night of March 30, 2013, certain he was going to have his work cut out for him against the red-hot Vancouver Canucks. Vancouver had not only arrived in Edmonton riding a six-game win streak, they had allowed just six goals over that stretch. But less than eight minutes after the opening faceoff, the Oilers had amassed a 4–0 lead, and Taylor Hall had eclipsed Wayne Gretzky's decades-old record for quickest hat trick to start a game.

"I've never been a part of anything like that before," said Dubnyk, who went on to finish with a 23-save shutout in the 4–0 victory. "It was 3–0 before I ever touched the puck. I'm thinking, *This is going to be good.*"

Hall needed just 7:53 to register his hat trick, bettering a record set by Gretzky in 1986 when he scored three in 12:38 to start a game. And it wasn't just a triumphant game for Hall; it was also a record-setting moment for the team. With two goals from Hall and a point shot from defenseman Ladislav Smid just 2:43 into the opening period, the Oilers also obliterated the team record for fastest three goals to start a game. The previous mark was 3:25, set back in 1981 in a game against the Colorado Avalanche. "Amazing start," said Smid after scoring his first goal of the season on a memorable night.

Hall opened the proceedings just 16 seconds in, then finished off his hat trick by threading a power-play goal past Roberto Luongo. "That's pretty cool. Any time you can break the Great One's record, it's pretty special," Hall said. "It was just one of those games where everything I shot at the start went in." He scored three goals on his first three shots.

"I never had a start like that," he continued. "I've had some hot starts with assists, but as far as goal scoring, and stuff going in right off the bat, I've never had that. It was definitely exciting. I don't think it'll ever happen again, but I'll definitely try."

By the time Gretzky was traded to the Los Angeles Kings, he had racked up 30 hat tricks in addition to nine four-goal games and four five-goal outings. Over his extraordinary career, he scored

Taylor Hall scores against Canucks goalie Roberto Luongo en route to a hat trick.

Enforcers Have Their Day

On Georges Laraque's official website—which is populated with all things Georges Laraque—there's a navigation link labeled *Hat Trick*. Yes, the night the Oilers enforcer scored three goals was a monumental moment, or as he put it: "It's not even a dream come true, because I never even thought about scoring three goals in one game."

Both Laraque and Dave Semenko—two of Edmonton's prized fighters—accomplished the improbable and registered hat tricks during their careers with the Oilers, pushing their way onto a long list of Edmonton players who have scored three or more goals.

Semenko, better known as Wayne Gretzky's tenacious guardian, had the score sheet covered in a 4–2 win over the New York Rangers on October 19, 1980, in Madison Square Garden. Fittingly, Gretzky assisted on all three goals.

Laraque, meanwhile, opened the scoring against the Los Angeles Kings on February 21, 2001, netting a Jim Dowd rebound before capping his night with a backhand. "I would never have thought I would see a hat on the ice for me. It's unbelievable," said the game's unlikely hero.

Both Semenko and Laraque are now lodged on a list with 14 other NHL enforcers who have netted three goals in a game—a list that includes the likes of Willi Plett, who registered his hat trick with the Calgary Flames during the 1981–82 season; the Detroit Red Wings' Darren McCarty; and the Philadelphia Flyers' Dave Schultz, who not only netted a pair of hat tricks but did so in the span of seven days.

Schultz, who still holds the league record for single-season penalty minutes at 472, registered his first three-goal game on January 3, 1974, against the New York Rangers, then repeated the feat against the Minnesota North Stars on January 10.

The most recent member of the club is Eric Boulton, who scored three for the Atlanta Thrashers in a 7–1 rout against the New Jersey Devils on December 18, 2010. He scored a career-high six goals that season.

More Quick Work from Hall

There aren't many of Wayne Gretzky's franchise records that will be eclipsed, but Taylor Hall managed to make one other addendum to the record book, scoring two goals in the lightning-quick span of eight seconds. In the opening period of a tilt in the timeworn Nassau Coliseum on October 17, 2013, Hall converted a feed from defenseman Justin Schultz, then netted a rebound in a 3–2 loss to the New York Islanders.

Gretzky scored two in *nine* seconds against the St. Louis Blues on February 18, 1981—a night on which he scored a franchise-high five goals in a 9–2 victory.

And as quick as Hall's eight seconds may be, it wasn't quick enough to better the NHL record, which stands at four seconds and is shared by Nels Stewart of the Montreal Maroons (1931) and the Winnipeg Jets' Deron Quint, who repeated the feat in a game against the Oilers in 1995.

Sheldon Souray and Ales Hemsky hold the Oilers record for two fastest goals by two players, which they set on November 23, 2009, in a game against the Phoenix Coyotes. They scored twice in seven seconds.

three or more goals in 50 games—another of his NHL records that may never be equaled.

Yet neither Gretzky nor Hall holds the record for fastest three goals in a game. Ryan Smyth needed just 2:01 to score his record-setting hat trick—an accomplishment achieved early in the third period of a 6–4 win over the San Jose Sharks in 2006.

70 Take a Road Trip

Not everyone possesses Rob Suggitt's scheduling wizardry, or his work flexibility, but count him among those who think it is worth checking out the view from a seat in another NHL arena. Suggitt, an Edmonton businessman, took a monthlong furlough in 2015 so he could travel from one NHL city to the next, taking in an astounding 30 games in 30 cities in 30 nights.

His self-funded adventure—which covered almost 40,000 kilometers—was part bucket list, part fund-raiser, and netted $43,000 for the Make-A-Wish Foundation. "I would map it out back in '07, '08 and think about doing it, then I'd change my mind. It's not a cheap trip to do…but I just procrastinated," he said. "It was the Make-A-Wish component that changed my mind."

Suggitt's 30-day expedition began on March 13, 2015, in Nassau Coliseum for a game between the New York Islanders and Ottawa Senators, and ended on April 11 in Toronto's Air Canada Center, where he was a guest for a tussle between the Maple Leafs and the Montreal Canadiens.

"Here's the amazing thing about that," he said. "We all know what travel delays are like, but I did 27 flights, two car rentals [because of the proximity], and one Amtrak, and my combined amount of travel delays amounted to four hours. That was sheer luck."

He continued, "Madison Square Garden is absolutely stunning. It was completely renovated in 2010–11, and people here know we spent about $450 million to build our arena…well, they spent $1 billion on the renovation. A *renovation*. And it's stunning. Marble floors. Wood grain everywhere. The only thing you can't do with a renovation, unfortunately, is make the concourses wider.

You go out during intermission, and it is shoulder to shoulder. Tighter than almost any arena I can remember, but that's New York. That's the way they walk down the street.

"And there's the history there too. Another thing people don't realize is that with all the money involved in hockey, there are only two arenas [that] don't sell the [naming rights]. Madison Square Garden is one of them. Joe Louis in Detroit is the other. Can you imagine what they could get for selling their naming rights? I think that's very cool."

Suggitt, who holds a quarter share of season tickets, was also won over by Rogers Place, which is just four blocks from his downtown office. "I try and be as objective as possible, but I do think it's the No. 1 arena in the NHL," he continued. "We went from 29th or even 30th to 1st. Let's hope the team can do that on the ice, but there's no other building like it."

Dennis Laliberte, president of Newwest Travel & Cruises, has been offering destination packages for several years and incorporates other sporting events as well. Among the many offerings, there's been an excursion to Green Bay, Wisconsin, for a Packers game after an Oilers-Blackhawks game and an Oilers-Stars game followed by a Dallas Cowboys game. The first trip was a jaunt to Boston for a playoff game in 1988.

"There were some down years, when the Oilers weren't all that popular. It wasn't until about six, seven years ago that we ramped it up," said Laliberte. And he's had regulars, such as Barry Hunka and his wife, Brenda, who have been on most of the trips.

"Favorite road arena? Madison Square Garden. And also the Staples Center," said Barry Hunka, from his office in Vegreville, Alberta. Season ticket holders since the 1990s, the couple also makes the hour-plus commute for the Oilers' home games.

While Phoenix, Anaheim, and Los Angeles are popular destinations for snowbound Oilers fans, there are other targets worth considering. Montreal may not be as appealing—weather-wise—as

Phoenix is in the middle of January, but the game presentation and the history are worth the trip. The same can be said for New York's Madison Square Garden.

"One thing I did learn on the trip is that getting a single ticket to any game was real easy," said Suggitt. "Example: Game 29. It was the last home game in Montreal, and as I was walking to the arena, I met a whole bunch of scalpers who said, 'You're not going to get a ticket. I walked to the box office at 2:00 on game day, and I could sit where I wanted to. If it was two or more tickets, it may be not as easy. But it was amazing to see the difference in price [from city to city]. Chicago was about the most expensive; New York was up there. But in Buffalo, I got two seats, row 15 or 16, right at center ice for $55 a ticket. Best seats in the house. There's a real disparity in ticket prices throughout the NHL."

Laliberte is a fan of MSG, Montreal's Bell Centre, and the Staples Center because of "its West Coast energy, laser light show. It's cranked up."

He added, "There's a lot of Oiler fans wherever we seem to go. They are all over the place now. Even in Montreal, we were quite surprised by the number of fans."

71 The Go-Between

Ask Jill Metz—the Oilers family liaison—what one of her days looks like, and she pauses. And pauses a little longer as she tries to catalog all her recent duties. She finally surrenders. There is no sameness in her role, which was added in the 2007–08 season when the Oilers started offering the service to their players. They were one of the first teams in the NHL to set up the position, and Metz has been their concierge from the get-go, fulfilling an assortment of requests.

Metz has been on call when an expectant mom has needed a helping hand, and she has been an emergency contact for Wiggles, the family dog. She has arranged driving exams for players and set up English lessons. She is a Jill-of-all-trades whose mission is to ease the challenges that come from moving to a new city, and in some cases, a new country.

When players are added to the team through a trade or free agency, Metz is on the phone with the new Oilers to find out whether or not they have a family, and what their needs might be. If they have children, she'll pass on the name of a pediatrician; if they need a realtor, she'll forward that info as well. She's discreet, enterprising, and often one of the last to leave the rink on game nights, as another of her roles is to host the hospitality rooms.

Every team has a team services expert who arranges air and ground transportation for the players and the coaches, as well as the hotel accommodations and catering needs when the team is on the road. Metz, meanwhile, stays much closer to home.

"It worked. It really did," said Patrick LaForge, president of the club when the position was added. "Players come from all over the world. We had Russians, we had Swedes, Finns and Czechs, and a lot of kids from the United States. College grads. Junior players. Everybody has [made] a real concerted effort to on-board new players in a whole different way. It was the right thing to do."

It was general manager Kevin Lowe, rebuffed by numerous free agents and their wives, who decided to mirror the methods of non-hockey corporations, and proposed the idea of bringing in a concierge. It was just one of the changes the Oilers had to make to try and better the reputation Edmonton had gotten as an NHL wasteland.

Transitioning players and their families into the community became a necessity, and Metz was recruited. She is their one-stop resource. One day, she'll be discussing menus for the family room at Rogers Place, the next she'll be rounding up parking passes and tickets. Or greeting a player's mom who just flew in. Or digging up the name of a landscaper, or shepherding the Oilers' ladies to a fund-raiser. "People always want to hear about my job because it is unique. It is a cool job," she said, "and I think that it demonstrates that our team cares about families."

Some even become her extended family. Over the years, Metz has been to weddings and baby showers...many baby showers. "You spend a lot of time with them," she said. "I spend more time with the team and their families than I do with my own friends during the hockey season."

72. Economy Class Citizens No More

The budget-conscious Oilers were one of the last NHL teams still flying commercial when the league issued a directive that all teams were to travel on charter flights. The ruling went into effect before 9/11 changed the way the world travels with increased airport security measures and restrictive carry-on baggage rules.

Traveling from Edmonton has always been particularly demanding, with few teams logging more air miles over the course of a season. But making the switch from commercial to charter aircrafts reduced the time the team spent in airports and eliminated the need to make connections while affording the players more room. The Canadian teams all fly on Air Canada's charter service, Jetz, which uses Airbus A319 aircraft with 58 business class seats.

Times have changed. Teams also pay heed to sleep studies, while some coaches even take into account time zone changes when they are mapping out practice schedules. Fitness coaches often travel with the teams, teams consult nutritionists, and there are mandated days off. It is a league requirement to give players a minimum of four days off a month, and there has to be a minimum of nine hours between the time their flight touches down and the start of their next practice when the team is on the road. Players are even flown to training camp in business class seats.

"Today's player has absolutely no idea what the players back then had to go through," said Todd Marchant, who played for the Oilers long enough that he flew both commercial and on the charters. "They were long travel days. If you went on an eight-day road trip, it felt like an eternity. You'd play that night, fly all the next day, then practice, play the next day, and do it all over again.

"But I will say this: I felt like the camaraderie amongst the players was greater than it is today. Now, I'm not in the dressing room and not traveling with the team as much; I just know that those times you spent together really made you bond as a group."

Some teams were not able to travel in the style they had grown accustomed to following the 2012 lockout because Air Canada had reconfigured their charter planes and put them back into regular service. There wasn't enough time to switch them all back in time for the start of the abbreviated 2012–13 season, and it did not sit well with some of the players. At least they didn't have to sit in the middle seats.

"When Billy Ranford got traded, I took over not only the player rep duties but the ticket duties," Marchant continued. "I used to have a little index card I carried with me, and at the beginning of the season, it would list everyone's name, the amount of games they'd played, and what they preferred: aisle or window. Then you had to determine whether the guy was in the card game…and you'd need maybe six aisle seats that were all together. Then you'd have middles. They'd go to the young guys, to the guys who were lowest on the totem pole. And as soon as you gave the guy the

In Memory

Garnet "Ace" Bailey, who played for the Oil Kings and the WHA Oilers, and scouted for Edmonton in the team's dynasty days, was among those killed in the September 11, 2001, terrorist attacks. That fateful day, the plane he was on, United Airlines Flight 175, was highjacked after takeoff from Boston's Logan Airport and flown into the World Trade Center in New York City.

Bailey, the Los Angeles Kings' director of pro scouting at the time, was traveling with Mark Bavis, another of the Kings' scouts. His life was also cut short by the incomprehensible tragedy. They were on their way to Los Angeles for the start of the Kings training camp.

When the Kings won their first Stanley Cup in 2012, family members of Bailey and Bavis, along with the members of the team's hockey operations department, made a trip to the 9/11 memorial in New York with the championship trophy.

ticket, he'd run to security and race to the gate to ask if there was any chance he could get out of the middle seat."

Marchant retired in 2011, after 18 seasons in the league, and moved into the role of director of player development for the Anaheim Ducks. He still travels, and not on a charter flight—which has revived memories of the old days.

One story revolves around Mike Stapleton, one of the Ducks' scouts, whom Marchant played with briefly in Edmonton. Marchant said, "We were on a flight when we were playing—I forget where we were going or coming from, but I'd gotten to the gate early, got out of my middle seat and into a window seat. It was perfect. Then all of a sudden, I got a tap on my shoulder, and it was [veteran] Mike Stapleton. He just said, 'This lady is at the back of the plane, in the last row, in the middle, and you're going to give her your seat.' What was I going to say? I was a young kid. So I moved.

"I'm laughing and smiling now because there were some good times...and we didn't know any different. But when you finish playing now, after let's say 10 years, and all of a sudden you say, 'I want to get a job as a scout,' well, you're not flying first class. It's a bit of a culture shock."

73 Passing the Bar

One of the quirky design elements in the Oilers' former home was a walkway that took the players from their locker room to the ice. Bordered by an ice-level lounge, it at times became an unavoidable collision course between underachieving team members and game patrons emboldened by alcohol. It became a gauntlet of sorts, with a cacophony of catcalls arising on more than one occasion.

"You have guys coming off the ice and people slurring, 'You suck,'" Shawn Horcoff said after he was traded to the Dallas Stars. "Man, that's tough. You go from being built up [on the ice] to exhaling [on the walk to the locker room]."

In his first year as general manager, Craig MacTavish got into a shouting match with a fan after a 5–2 loss to the St. Louis Blues. He said later that it was the usual stuff but that he had had enough. So too had the fans. With the Oilers taking up residence at the bottom of the league standings for several seasons, fans started tossing their jerseys onto the ice.

"You're a fan, you get to say and do whatever you want. Call me whatever name you want, but when it comes to that logo, that's a sacred thing for us," goaltender Ben Scrivens said after an 8–1 loss to the Calgary Flames in March 2014. He picked up a jersey that had been tossed onto the ice and launched it back into the stands. "It's disheartening for me to see our fans treat it that way."

Others concocted alternative tactics to voice their displeasure, such as the frustrated season-ticket holder who turned to Kijiji—a free classified site in Canada—to unload some tickets. Rather than attend a January game against the Columbus Blue Jackets, he traded a pair of $470 tickets for a case of Coors Light and a dog-grooming session. He had had his sights set on a bottle of Crown Royal.

As for the gauntlet, it is no more. In the Oilers' swanky new quarters, the players get to the ice though a private corridor.

74 Minor League Moments

Have a parrot sing the national anthem? Check. *Seinfeld* night with puffy shirt jerseys? Check. Offer Canadian singer Justin Bieber a contract? That too was one of the promos hatched by the Bakersfield Condors. The Condors were one of the most innovative minor league teams when it came to cooking up in-game promotions, an approach that had to be dialed down when the franchise was promoted from the ECHL to the American Hockey League.

The Oilers purchased the Condors, their ECHL farm team, in 2014. A year later, they ended their five-year affiliation agreement with the Oklahoma City Barons, flipped the Condors to the American Hockey League, and set off in the nearly realigned Western Conference that featured a Pacific Division for the five new California-based teams.

"At the beginning you do jersey giveaways and things like that to draw fans out and to draw families out," Matthew Riley, the president of the Condors, once said of Bakersfield's publicity efforts. As he told the Oilers website, there were not enough hockey fans in the community to sustain the business. They had to make the games an event. "After a while, you keep pushing the envelope and do more things," Riley said. "We were the first team to do a Mr. Potato Head giveaway where he was dressed in hockey gear and he had a black eye."

To salute Bakersfield High School grad Jake Varner's gold medal win at the London 2012 Summer Olympics, jerseys were created for his tribute night. They looked like wrestling singlets, complete with craftily created muscles and a gold medal. To commemorate the 150th anniversary of Abraham Lincoln's Gettysburg Address, another specially designed jersey was added to the franchise's expanding collection. And it wasn't all about jerseys. One game-goer once left with a cemetery plot from a giveaway. "There are very few things everyone will need eventually. This is something everyone needs," Riley told Yahoo! Sports about that gravesite. "We don't take ourselves too seriously. We're all about having fun."

Just for good, wacky measure, an Andean condor named Queen Victoria was once brought out to the ice at the Rabobank Arena in downtown Bakersfield for the anthem, but it got away from its handler and created all kinds of havoc, particularly when it flew into the team's bench. The video clip is a staple on blooper reels.

The marketing department drummed up a dandy when they staged a *Seinfeld* night. Not only did the players wear jerseys with puffy shirts, with names such as Kramer and Assman on the backs, there was a Festivus pole prize, a chuck-a-puck contest, and a dance-off—Elaine Benes style, of course.

After Michael Jackson passed away, the Condors didn't just honor the King of Pop with alternate jerseys styled to resemble the trademark red jacket he once wore, each of the players' right gloves was white.

When Charlie Sheen was dominating the entertainment news, the Condors declared if anyone could come up with the $2 million salary the *Two and a Half Men* star was collecting per episode, they could own the ECHL team outright.

Anyone who provided a clean drug test received free admission, and two Tiger Blood Icees could be had for the price of one.

When the 2012 NHL lockout was looming, they proclaimed on their website that they had offered Bieber an amateur contract. "I've scouted some video of him online, skating with my hometown team, the Toronto Maple Leafs, and I think he could provide some elusive speed up front for us," head coach / director of hockey operations Matt O'Dette was quoted as saying. "Plus, he's a right-handed shot, which we've been looking to add."

That was then. For their first home game in the AHL, the first 5,000 game-goers received a pair of sunglasses. The thought behind that promo? "Our future is so bright, we gotta wear shades."

75 The Long Good-Bye

The game had ended hours earlier, but Ryan Smyth, still susceptible to surges of sentimentality, did not want the night to end. It was 1:38 AM before the 38-year-old winger finally took off his jersey and his equipment, officially marking the end of his career. "I still get emotional when I talk about it," said Smyth, who for so many years was the heart and soul of the franchise. "I knew it was going to be hard; I didn't think it was going to be that tough, but [it was] a pretty special moment for myself and my family. What a great send-off."

Days before the Oilers closed out the 2013–14 season at home against the Vancouver Canucks, Smyth announced it would be the last game of his career. He had lost the foot race with Father

Time, but that didn't make it any easier to leave behind a career that spanned 18 seasons and embodied 1,270 regular-season games—971 as an Oiler, which left him trailing only team leader Kevin Lowe (1,037).

Before the game against the Vancouver Canucks got under way, Smyth was presented with a jersey that had been stitched with a C—the same jersey he didn't want to take off. Throughout the emotional night, there were messages interspersed on the scoreboard from former teammates, as well as highlights. And tears... lots of tears.

His parents, Jim and Dixie, were in the crowd, as was his wife, Stacey, and their four children. There were thank-you signs in the stands, thank-yous from the four on-ice officials. The Canucks, in an unexpected show of respect, came back out on the ice too, just to shake his hand.

"I didn't leave the rink until about 2:00, and there were still fans around...pretty cool to see," said Smyth, who left with all kinds of scars to show for all the years he'd parked himself in front of an opponent's net.

His was not only a memorable exit after 18 years in the league, it was about the only memorable moment from an otherwise dismal season. All that was missing was a power-play goal from the gritty veteran, who needed just one more to supplant Glenn Anderson as the team's all-time leader. They are both in the Oilers record book with 126.

"I think he embodies what the Edmonton fans like in a hockey player," said goaltender Ben Scrivens. "He's a never-say-quit, go-to-the-tough-areas, score-a-goal-with-your-face-if-you-have-to type of player. I think that resonates with the people around here."

Retirement did not sit well with Smyth. It took almost a year before he really started to emerge from his malaise, and then he found his way to the ice with the Stony Plain Eagles in the Chinook Hockey League, just to fill his hockey void.

He became a minority owner of the Junior A Spruce Grove Saints, joined Hockey Canada's under-18 management team, and in 2016 played for the alumni team in the Heritage Classic in Winnipeg, alongside the likes of Wayne Gretzky, Mark Messier, Glenn Anderson, and Jari Kurri.

"I can't believe he was able to keep himself composed because I think everyone in the room was ready to tear up with him," David Perron said after Smyth told his former teammates he was done. The biggest [message was that] it's hard to play in this league; it's even harder when you leave."

Selected sixth overall in 1994, the Banff native idolized Gretzky, grew up watching the Oilers, and was a regular at Glen Sather's hockey school in the mountain community. It was only fitting he would play his last game as an Oiler, in Edmonton, after seasons with the New York Islanders and Los Angeles Kings. Traded to the Islanders in 2007, after contract negotiations came to a standstill, Smyth asked the Kings to trade him back to the Oilers four years later.

"He was a guy who had an amazing amount of passion for the game, and you learn from that as a young player," said former teammate Sam Gagner. "You see the way he competes, even through adversity, and all the things he does to make himself a better player. He's left such a lasting impression."

76 An Endurance Test

It began as a labor of love, this spectacle called the World's Longest Game—a tribute to the father who once told Brent Saik, "Make sure that no kids ever go into this hospital." Saik, an optometrist whose client list includes the Oilers, lost both his dad, Terry, and later his wife, Susan, to cancer, and he has made it his mission to raise funds to help in the ongoing fight against the disease.

At the heart of his fund-raising is a marathon hockey game that has since found its place in the *Guinness Book of World Records*. A dedicated, if not somewhat daffy, group of 40 hockey players played for 250 hours, 3 minutes, and 20 seconds in a marathon that began on February 6, 2015, and ended 10 days later.

"Brent told me the best thing. He told me that we are not actually playing hockey, we're inspiring people. That's my motto," said Janne Niinimaa, the former Oilers defenseman who made the trip over from Finland to take part in the longest game. Getting into the record book was never Saik's focus. The objective of his first longest game was to raise money for the Alberta Cancer Foundation. Four other games followed.

In their then-record-setting outing in 2015, the group raised more than $1.2 million, pushing their cumulative total close to the $4 million mark. The outdoor game has been one of the most successful fund-raising events for the cancer foundation.

All the players have their reasons for playing, and it is what keeps them going during the longest hours of the longest game. "When people come to play here, it's because they're playing for loved ones," Saik said in an interview with NHL.com. He organized the Terry Saik Memorial Golf Tournament in 1996 and his first hockey game in 2003. Susan was diagnosed after that first game.

"Every single player in every single game has cried at some point—at least once. Usually 10 times. It's a beautiful, beautiful room where people can tell their stories. You realize how important life is, and what's important," Saik said.

Saik smiles before the record-setting World's Longest Hockey Game gets under way.

The hockey game takes place on Saik's property outside Edmonton—better known as Saiker's Acres. He's since added a 7,700-square-foot, two-story facility to accommodate dressing rooms for the players, medical facilities, and a viewing area for fans. Shifts are four hours long, which is the longest shift permitted by Guinness. Players also have to remain on-site in order for the record to stand. "The first two or three days are usually pure hell," said Jouni Nieminen, one of five players who has played in all five games. "Somehow your body gets used to it, which I could never understand. I've seen guys play in that game with injuries that just freak me out. I have been lucky."

The event has grown significantly since 2003, when the weekend warriors played for 82 hours and raised $150,000, money that was used to purchase a gene analyzer for pediatric cancer research. On top of the 40 players who took part in the record-setting game in 2015, there were 81 referees, 46 scorekeepers, and 50 volunteer massage therapists.

In the fall of 2016, Saik introduced the World's Longest Baseball Game, which required 56 players who were intent on breaking the record of 70:09:24 set in Sauget, Illinois, on May 24, 2015. Hampered by rain, cool temperatures, and some tournament-ending injuries, including a broken foot and a torn Achilles' tendon, the group played 237 innings over 72 hours and raised $250,000.

77 Eight Was Enough

It was the quintessential start to another February game for the hapless Oilers. Down 2–0 to the dynamic Chicago Blackhawks early in the second period, there was no reason to think that on the night of February 2, 2012, another entry was going to be scribbled into the record book. Particularly not by Sam Gagner, who had gone into the game with just five goals and 22 points.

But minutes into the middle frame, Gagner sent Taylor Hall in on a breakaway with a long pass. Minutes later, he picked up his own rebound, curled around the net, and scored on a wraparound. What followed was remarkable. Gagner, then 22, finished with four goals and eight points in an 8–4 victory, tying Wayne Gretzky and Paul Coffey, who had both registered eight-point nights for the Oilers decades before. In fact, more than 23 years had passed since any player in the NHL had put up eight points in a regular-season game. (The league record is 10 points, set by the Toronto Maple Leafs' Darryl Sittler on February 7, 1976.)

"I think maybe in minor hockey I had eight, but that's going a long way back," Gagner said after his historic night. "I didn't think I had that good of a first period. After that, it seemed that everything I touched was going in."

Gretzky, one of 11 players to register eight points in a regular-season game, first accomplished the feat in a 13–4 win over the New Jersey Devils on November, 19, 1983 (three goals, five assists), then repeated it again on January 4, 1984, in a 12–8 win over the Minnesota Wild (four goals, four assists). Coffey scored two goals and assisted on six others on March 14, 1986, in a 12–3 win over the Detroit Red Wings. All three Oilers registered their eight-point nights on home ice.

"I had 60 [texts and emails] last night, and another 50 when I got up this morning…a couple of really big ones too," Gagner said. "Wayne Gretzky texted me. Paul Coffey as well. To be mentioned in a record with those guys is a pretty special feeling."

His was the first eight-point night in an NHL regular-season game since December 31, 1988, when Mario Lemieux of the Pittsburgh Penguins scored five goals and assisted on three others in an 8–6 win over the New Jersey Devils.

"It's a lot harder to get eight points in a month [in today's NHL], let alone in one night," said Ron Wilson, who was coaching the Maple Leafs in 2012.

"Some guys don't touch the puck eight times in a game," Leafs forward Joffrey Lupul marveled after Gagner's big night.

By the time Gagner had scored his fourth goal, hats were in short supply, so one game-goer threw a shoe onto the ice. "I was hoping that would be the end of it, because if he scored another one, we might have seen other paraphernalia out there," said head coach Tom Renney. "It puts a smile on your face during a tough year."

Gagner, who scored the four goals on six shots and racked up all eight points in less than 35 minutes, didn't cool off immediately either. Two nights later, in a 5–4 shootout win over the Detroit Red Wings, he scored twice and registered an assist in the first period. In short, he had a hand in 11 straight Edmonton goals—a new club record. Gretzky had contributed to 10 consecutive goals in 1984, and again in 1986. Gagner finished the season with 18 goals and 47 points; the Oilers finished 29th.

78 The Hot Hand

Almost 5,000 overtime games had been played in the NHL when a rookie with fleet feet and hot hands scripted a new league record by scoring the winning goals in three straight overtime games. It was a magic moment for Andrew Cogliano, who entered the record book for what he had accomplished between March 7 and March 11, 2008. "Unbelievable," he said after scoring his third game winner and before the Hockey Hall of Fame called to ask for his Easton stick.

Cogliano's heroics began on a snowy March night in Columbus, Ohio, where the Oilers had relinquished a 1–0 lead with just more than one second left in regulation. Enter the rookie, who whipped the deciding goal through the legs of Pascal Leclaire. Two days later, in Chicago's United Center, in a rare afternoon contest, the Toronto native scored in regulation then tapped the overtime winner past goaltender Patrick Lalime to lift the Oilers to a 6–5 win over the Blackhawks. When the team returned to Rexall Place to host the St. Louis Blues, the 20-year-old freshman was at it again, this time beating Manny Legace, with just 4.9 seconds left on the clock, to become the first player in league history to score the game winner in three consecutive games.

Cogliano also tied the NHL record for most overtime goals in a season by a rookie, joining the Pittsburgh Penguins' Ryan Malone (2003–04) and Sidney Crosby (2005–06). All three have since been trumped by Philadelphia Flyers defenseman Shayne Gostisbehere, who netted four in his rookie season in 2015–16. But that was after the NHL introduced three-on-three play in overtime. Crosby, Malone, and Cogliano scored at a time when overtime was still four-on-four. More telling, however, is this: between the time the

NHL introduced sudden-death overtime in 1983–84 and the night of March 11, 2008, when Cogliano notched his third straight, a total of 4,924 games required extra time.

"It's quite a story," Oilers coach Craig MacTavish said of Cogliano's feat. "Add that to the list of wild and wacky things that you see over the years that really defy all odds or any explanation. That's why people play the lottery. Sometimes it happens."

A late first-round selection of the Oilers in the 2005 draft, Cogliano was eventually traded to the Anaheim Ducks, where he has continued to make news. He scored his first career hat trick by netting three straight goals in the second period of a 4–1 win over the Phoenix Coyotes on January 31, 2012. It took him just 6:51 to score the three goals—the second-fastest hat trick in Ducks history. And it was a natural; no empty nets. A year later, he scored three again. Again against the Coyotes. And again against Mike Smith.

But his accomplishments didn't end there. Cogliano, at 5'10" and 184 pounds, has been so tough, so durable, so willful that he became only the second NHL player to start his career by playing 700 straight games. (The first player to play 700 straight from the start of his career was Doug Jarvis, the league's leading ironman, who played 964 straight games during a career that started with the Montreal Canadiens in 1975 and ended with the Hartford Whalers in 1988.) Cogliano played his 700th consecutive game on April 3,

Working Overtime

In 2004, for a record-setting stretch of seven games, the Oilers were involved in an overtime contest. Between February 29 and March 12, they lost third-period leads, erased deficits, and registered a record of 2–2–3 before ending the streak with a 3–1 regulation victory over the Ottawa Senators. "Seven overtimes…that's enough," proclaimed Radek Dvorak.

Seven teams had held the previous record, which was five straight overtime games.

2016—putting him on a pretty exclusive list; only five other players in league history have passed the 700-game milestone. Cogliano, who played his first 328 games with the Oilers, moved into fifth place on the all-time list during the 2016–17 season.

79 A Wing and a Prayer

The clutching and grabbing was incessant, annoyingly so. But Wayne Gretzky couldn't control himself. Neither could Sean Brown or Rod Phillips. All three were frightfully fearful of flying. Every takeoff, every landing, every unsteady movement was troublesome, which was an issue given how often the team was in the air. Few teams, then or now, travel more miles in a season than the Oilers.

Phillips, the longtime voice of the team's broadcasts, and Gretzky, the team's star center, often sat side by side on commercial flights. "Gretz will tell you I was the one who made him a bad flyer. I don't know about that," said Phillips. "But I would sit on the window seat, he would sit in the middle seat…and we said our final good-byes many, many times when we were flying through storms or coming in for bad landings."

Brown didn't join the Oilers until 1998, but his unease at 30,000 feet was as widely recognized. "You know if you're sitting beside him, you're not going to sleep much," teammate Domenic Pittis once said of Brown's anxiety.

Brown, a 6'3", 205-pound defenseman, wouldn't flinch at the prospect of a scrap on the ice, but when it came to flying, his fortitude evaporated. He suffered through it, tried to beat the fear down, but if the plane hit turbulence, he'd be grabbing onto the seat, or a seatmate. "Everybody has a fear of something; mine just happens to be flying," he said. "I'll conquer it. It will never get to the point where I'm not going to get on a plane."

Gretzky was eventually able to temper his fear, but it took some work. He visited a hypnotherapist, which worked for a time. He took mind-control classes too, but it was a trip to the cockpit that finally started him on his road to recovery. Once he saw all the dials, knobs, and switches, and the control the pilots had, he had a breakthrough. He knew he wasn't claustrophobic; he just couldn't handle the bumpy rides. He became a regular in the cockpit. "I may be the only guy in the NHL who wants to go back to the days of the six-team NHL," he said in his early years with the Oilers. "Remember, they rode trains."

As for Phillips, he never did get comfortable in his window seat, not even when the team started flying charter. "I don't fly that much anymore, but I'm still not a good flyer," said Phillips, who called his last game in 2011. He drives to the desert in the winters now and watches the Oilers on the television—with his feet firmly planted on the ground. "I felt so much stress that in 2010 I just decided it wasn't good for me anymore," he said. "I was still relatively young, I was 68 at the time, but [my dislike of flying] was the main reason I retired."

80 Mistaken Identity

There are numerous spelling gaffes, spacing errors, and snafus on the Stanley Cup, which is still engraved by hand:

After the Oilers laid claim to their first Stanley Cup, Peter Pocklington added his father, Basil, to the list of names to be

Cup Facts

Championship teams are allowed to have 52 names engraved, and with the passage of time, as more silver bands have been added, some have had to be removed. One comes off every 13 years and is safeguarded in the Hockey Hall of Fame. It is the only trophy on which the name of every team member is inscribed.

The bowl perched at the top of the Stanley Cup is a copy. The original trophy was a punch bowl that was just 7.28 inches high. Purchased in 1892 for 10 guineas (the equivalent of $50) by Sir Frederick Arthur, the Lord Stanley of Preston, it has undergone several alterations: Tiered rings were added, as were long narrow rings. The original bowl was removed in 1962 because it had become too fragile, and was replaced by a replica. The original bowl and the retired name bands are on display at the Hockey Hall of Fame. And when the original Stanley Cup is out on tour, or at an arena in advance of a championship presentation, a replica sits in its display case. The replica does not sport the original's mistakes.

engraved on the coveted trophy. When league officials later determined Basil had nothing to do with the team, a decree came down that his name was to be struck. It took 16 X's to cover it up.

One of the early mistakes can be found on the entry for the 1941–42 Toronto Maple Leafs. Turk Broda is listed twice: once as Turk Broda and once as Walter Broda.

The Leafs' Gaye Stewart had his name spelled *Gave* while the team name was misspelled Toronto Maple *Leaes* after the club's 1962–63 victory.

The Bruins were listed as *Bqstqn Bruins* in 1972.

Frank Selke was the Maple Leafs' assistant manager in 1945, and his title on the Cup reads *ass man*.

The engraving celebrating the New York Islanders' 1980–81 victory was botched as well. It reads *Ilanders*.

Goaltender Jacques Plante had his name misspelled four times in five years.

Speaking of Trophies...

One of Gretzky's diversions back in the 1990s was his Canadian Football League partnership with John Candy, the late Canadian comedian, and Kings owner Bruce McNall. The three had a stake in the Toronto Argonauts, though Candy and Gretzky were minority owners, so their names were not engraved on the trophy when the Argos won the Grey Cup in 1991. Both their names were later added in 2007.

Candy was in the process of securing control of the team when he died on a movie set in Mexico on March 4, 1994.

Manny Legace, a goaltender with the 2002 Stanley Cup champions from Chicago, was listed as *Lagace*, a mistake that was later corrected by the engraver.

Eric Staal was Eric *Staaal* after the Carolina Hurricanes win in 2006. Again, a mistake that was corrected.

The Blackhawks' Kris Versteeg's name was corrected after the team's 2009–10 win. It initially read, *Vertseeg*.

81 The House Gretzky Did Not Build

Directly east of Rogers Place sits the Brewery District, a shopping destination that has risen from the remains of a historic brewery. It was also the former home of Molson House, an adjoining log reception hall that played host to countless press conferences—not the least of which was the August 9, 1988, gathering at which Oilers owner Peter Pocklington announced Wayne Gretzky had been traded to the Los Angeles Kings.

The Edmonton Brewing and Malting Company Building opened in 1913—a building that cost $610,000 to build and was so ornate that locals once called it the Oliver Beer Castle. It continued to stand on 104th Avenue and 121st Street after it was purchased by Molson in 1958.

Molson closed the brewery in 2007, at a time when the demand for canned beer products trumped bottled products. A labor impasse also factored into the decision to close the plant—which produced only bottled beer—leaving 136 employees out of work. What remains of the original brewery today is the historic Molson tower and the red bricks that were salvaged from the old brewery—bricks that were baked with Edmonton-mined coal.

Molson House was added to the property in 1961, after Molson acquired it. Designed to resemble a fur trade fort, the wooden structure housed a reception room that was used by the brewery to entertain customers and host numerous other gatherings. In 2002 several of the Oilers gathered there to watch Canada defeat the US in the Olympic gold medal hockey game. If the Coliseum was the House That Gretzky Built, Molson House was the House where the Oilers were dismantled.

So before Molson Canada put the brewery site up for sale, they let it be known they were willing to donate Molson House to a community group that was willing to dismantle the building and reassemble it elsewhere. Otherwise, it was going to be torn down.

"We just thought that [since] people had expressed that they had lots of fond memories of Molson House and that it was, to some degree, a hospitality institution, we might as well put the word out [in case] anyone [had] an interest," Ferg Devins, the company's vice president of public affairs said. There were some tire kickers, even the Valley Zoo considered using the building as a clubhouse in the children's area, but in the end, there were no takers.

Fast-forward to 2010. At the 11th hour, with construction to begin at the site, Molson House was sold to an Edmonton family who had it moved to a location just outside the city. The family wanted to remain anonymous.

82 Tough as Nails

As linesman Jay Sharrers was scooping up three of Ryan Smyth's lower front teeth, which were scattered on the ice—one with a root attached—the winger was making his way to the medical room to have his bloody mouth repaired. Smacked in the face by a Chris Pronger clearing pass in Game 3 of the 2006 conference semifinals, Smyth not only returned to the ice after eight stitches had been woven into his lacerated lip, he scored the game winner in a 3–2 triple-overtime victory over the San Jose Sharks.

There's never been a shortage of tenacious titans in the game. Before the Oilers reached the playoffs in 2006, Marty Reasoner was struck by a puck on the right side of his head, and after 30 jagged stitches were knit into his puffy, blood-red ear, he returned to the ice.

Wipe the blood, stitch the wound, get back on the ice. Iron men with iron wills. Kevin Lowe was no exception, playing with broken ribs and a fractured wrist in the 1988 playoffs. Lee Fogolin once popped a crown off an abscessed tooth with a hanger he'd grabbed out of the hotel closet because he didn't want to miss a game.

The hard-hitting Mike Grier dislocated his right shoulder in 2000–01 but wouldn't leave the lineup, choosing instead to put off surgery until after the season. Routinely, he needed to have the shoulder popped back into place. "He played two years in a harness," said Ken Lowe, the club's longtime medical trainer. "I never had to push a guy out onto the ice. It was always more about pulling them off."

Defenseman Igor Ulanov's toughness was almost as mythic as the steely reputation of defenseman Jason Smith. The two unflinching shot blockers once sat side by side with their mangled feet submerged in a bucket of ice. "There are mornings when you're aching and paining a little bit, but it's just a matter of getting used to it," the understated Smith said during his playing days. "I just try and go about doing what I can to help the team."

Battered, bruised, and bloodied, Oilers players have continually shown grit on the ice. Here, center Ryan Nugent-Hopkins takes one for the team in 2017.

Ulanov once took a puck in the forehead and needed 22 stitches to close the gash over the golf ball–sized knot on his forehead. He returned to finish the game and was on the ice the next afternoon for a team practice.

"It's just the mentality guys have. You are caught up in the emotion of the game and you want to get out there as soon as possible," Reasoner said back in 2006, when he returned to the ice with what his head coach, Craig MacTavish, referred to as a "Civil War bandage" over his fresh wound. "It's something you grow up with. It's obviously not going to be comfortable and it's not going to feel great, but once you realize it's not really, really serious, you just want to patch it up and get back out."

That same season, Reasoner was hit so hard in the chest with a puck that he was left with a bruised lung. He took a puck in the forehead, another on a hand, then the shot in the ear, which came off Pronger's stick.

Overexposure

Sergei Zholtok had only been with the Oilers for a couple weeks when he limped into the treatment room the morning after he'd injured his foot blocking a shot. Following his treatment session, medical trainer Ken Lowe told Zholtok to put on his skate because he needed to see if he'd be able to get back onto the ice once his injured foot was compressed into the boot.

"He looked at me like I had two heads. But he put his skate on and looked stunned that he could walk. Then I said, 'One last thing. I want you to go out and just skate.' Now he's really giving me the look," Lowe said. "It wasn't because he didn't want to test it. I had forgotten it was an open practice, and he was in his underwear. There were 5,000 people sitting in their seats, and he's out there skating around in his underwear. I felt so bad."

Zholtok, acquired by Edmonton in a late-season trade with the Montreal Canadiens, played 37 games with the Oilers before he was dealt to the Minnesota Wild. Tragically, his heart gave out in 2004 while he was playing for Riga, in his hometown of Latvia. He was 31.

Lowe spent years putting the players back together, after stepping into the role of medical trainer in 1989. Before he joined the Oilers, he worked with the Edmonton Eskimos. He's seen it all—dislocated joints, broken bones, bloody wounds. He has also had to advise players when it's time to sit out of the lineup.

During the Oilers last Stanley Cup run, when Dwayne Roloson was driven into his goal post, Lowe knew the goaltender's playoffs were over. "He didn't know he'd hurt his knee. He had hit his elbow against the post and he thought he broke his arm," said Lowe. "All he had done was hit the ulnar nerve—the funny bone—but then I said to him, 'Butterfly for me.' As soon as he went down, you could see the look on his face."

During the course of an 82-game season, players are often pulled out of the lineup to speed up the healing process. During a playoff run, that isn't the case. If they can play, they will play. "Everyone downgraded whatever it was," said Lowe. "Many times it was a case of us having to say no to them. You don't get to [the NHL] without a pain threshold that is well above that of the average person."

83 Save This Moment

There were no attention-getting indications of what was to come the night Ben Scrivens redrafted two entries in the record books. He had stopped 10 pucks in the warm-up by his estimation. Ten. At the most. And he was about to face the San Jose Sharks, who sauntered into Edmonton averaging 2.96 goals per game. Moreover, it was only his fourth game with the Oilers following his trade from the Los Angeles Kings. In short, Scrivens had left a team that had the stingiest defense in the NHL for a team with the league's highest goals-against average. The Oilers had given up 4 or more goals in 8 of their previous 10 games.

Yet he went out and set up shop in the net on January 29, 2014, and turned in an astounding 59-save performance in a 3–0 win over the Sharks. It was the most saves in franchise history—surpassing the previous mark of 56 recorded by Bill Ranford in a 4–3 overtime win over the New York Rangers on March 17, 1993. It was also a new NHL record for saves in a regular-season shutout. The previous mark was 54 saves by the Phoenix Coyotes' Mike Smith on April 3, 2012.

"I had an awful, awful warm-up, so it was an inauspicious start," Scrivens said after his goaltending clinic against the Sharks, "but it was one of those things where you try not to look at the forest while you're in the trees. You just try and focus on the process."

He made 20 saves in the first 20 minutes and another 22 in the second period, which earned him a standing ovation and bettered his career high of 40 saves in a game. There was another rousing round of applause at game's end, in addition to the platitudes from across the ice.

"Heck of a performance," said Todd McLellan, then the coach of the Sharks. "In all my years in the league, I don't think I've seen that, so [I] give him credit."

Working Overtime...and Then Some

Ben Scrivens' 59-save performance is worth honoring, to be sure, but how about the work of Detroit Red Wings goaltender Normie Smith on March 24, 1936? In a playoff game between his Red Wings and the Montreal Maroons, the teams found themselves deadlocked through regulation, setting the stage for what would become the longest game in league history. It took six overtime periods before the Wings' Modere "Mud" Bruneteau scored at 2:25 AM—176 minutes and 30 seconds after the opening faceoff. Smith made 92 saves.

"That was the best goaltending performance I've ever seen," Ryan Nugent-Hopkins said that night. "It was just an outstanding game."

The Sharks had another 22 shots blocked and missed 19 attempts, ratcheting their total of shots on Edmonton's net to 100. "It was one of those nights," said Scrivens, who accomplished his feat in Edmonton's Rexall Place, a stone's throw from his hometown of Spruce Grove. "I owe the shot keeper a beer, I think."

There weren't many high points during Scrivens' tenure with the Oilers, save for his out-of-this-world performance against San Jose. There weren't many high points for the Oilers, either, particularly in net. Edmonton opened the 2013–14 season with Devan Dubnyk, who was traded to the Nashville Predators in order to acquire Scrivens, and Jason LaBarbera, who was put on waivers before the Oilers signed out-of-work free agent Ilya Bryzgalov. He was dealt to the Minnesota Wild later that same season, and Victor Fasth was picked up in a deal with the Anaheim Ducks.

Scrivens, meanwhile, got a two-year, $4.6 million contract extension from the Oilers two months after his game against San Jose, and went on to play a total of 78 games for Edmonton. Dispatched to the American Hockey League Bakersfield Condors to start the 2015–16 season, in favor of Cam Talbot, Scrivens was eventually traded to the Montreal Canadiens. He then spent the 2016–17 season with Dinamo Minsk in Russia's Kontinental Hockey League.

84 Long Droughts, Short Good-Byes

Of all the records the Oilers hold, one of the most disparaging marks is their absence from the playoffs. After advancing to Game 7 in the Stanley Cup Finals against the Carolina Hurricanes on June 19, 2006, the Oilers didn't appear in a playoff game until April 12, 2017, when they hosted the San Jose Sharks. That 10-season drought equals the league record first established by the Florida Panthers, who were absent from the playoffs from 2001 to 2011.

"You think about the number of guys who have [come] through and left, mostly based on the team's lack of success," said Jordan Eberle after the Oilers secured a berth in the 2017 playoffs and before they went on to finish eighth in the NHL, second in their division. "So it's been bittersweet that it took this long."

During the dry decade in Edmonton, player turnover was routine, and the door to the head coach's office revolved regularly, which was just another barometer of the bungles. But if there was a paragon for management's missteps, that honor may very well belong to Ralph Krueger, who had been hired by ousted GM Steve Tambellini. He was head coach for the 46 games played during the lockout-shortened 2012–13 season and guided the Oilers to a 19–22–7 campaign. The club was 24th overall—their best finish since 2008–09—yet two months later, he was fired…via Skype.

General manager Craig MacTavish cut ties with Krueger after interviewing Dallas Eakins, then the head coach of the Toronto Marlies. Instead of hiring Eakins for the associate coach position, MacTavish named him head coach, citing philosophical differences with Krueger. He felt Eakins' style was more in line with the way he wanted to run the team.

Coaching Carousel

2008–09: Craig MacTavish, who had held the post for eight years. Prior to that, the Oilers had eight coaches in the span of 21 seasons—and that includes a return engagement of Glen Sather in the 1993–94 season.

2009–10: Pat Quinn

2010–11: Tom Renney

2011–12: Tom Renney

2012–13: Ralph Krueger

2013: Dallas Eakins

2014–15: Dallas Eakins, until he was fired on December 15, 2015. Todd Nelson was then called up from the American Hockey League and named interim head coach for the duration of the season. Nelson left for the Detroit Red Wings organization after the Oilers hired Todd McLellan, and stepped in as head coach of the Grand Rapid Griffins.

2015–16: Todd McLellan was named the 14th head coach of the franchise on May 19, 2015.

"Obviously, I was a mismatch, because we were moving on the hockey side in the right direction," Krueger told ESPN.com a few years later. "There was no question the group was just beginning to jell out of that lockout season. And the organization decided to go with a different style of leadership.

"But the world has been kind to me after that. I would say I was just a cultural mismatch to where that club wanted to go."

He was quickly recruited by Mike Babcock, the coach of Canada's Olympic team, to work as an adviser for the 2014 Winter Games in Sochi, Russia. Shortly after Canada's gold medal run, he was hired by the Southampton Football Club, where he is serving as chairman of the English Premier League.

Krueger did return to hockey in the fall of 2016 to run the bench for Team Europe's entry in the World Cup of Hockey. He had players from eight countries, many of whom had never played together, and coaxed the underdogs to the final, where they were eventually trumped by Canada for the inaugural tournament title.

"I can't say enough good things about him," defenseman Christian Ehrhoff said.

"I think he's shown what a smart hockey brain he is," said center Frans Nielsen.

Krueger, a Winnipeg-born, European-schooled hockey coach, was running the national program in Switzerland when he was hired by the Oilers to work as Tom Renney's associate coach in 2010. Extremely versatile, he founded his own speakers bureau, authored a bestseller, and even worked for Dow Jones of Switzerland—all in addition to serving as a member of the World Economic Forum's council on new models of leadership since 2011. In short, he's accomplished. He gets things done.

"I would have loved to finish the story with the Oilers—that was the plan at the time. But they chose a different path, and I never had any hard feelings about that," Krueger said during the World Cup. "I was grateful for the experience. The way these players function nowadays, and the big business they are as individuals, and managing that properly, the NHL truly paved the way for me…I would never say never to coming back to hockey, but at this moment in time, this World Cup couldn't be a more perfect gig. To be able to jump back into hockey for a month, I'm like a kid in a candy store."

"I wouldn't be surprised if someone called him," Nielsen said. "I think they should. He showed how smart he is. He sees what kind of players and potential he has on his team, and he builds his system around that."

85 The Injury Bug Bit Hard

The sequence of events kept the Oilers in stitches, and not the kind of stitches caused by a good belly-splitting laugh. We're talking about the sutures, stitches, and staples needed to close wounds and surgical incisions. Among the issues plaguing the Oilers during their calamitous 2009–10 campaign were the illnesses and injuries that sent one player after another into the medical room.

Center Mike Comrie missed 35 games with mononucleosis, goaltender Nikolai Khabibulin required back surgery, defenseman Sheldon Souray left the lineup after breaking his hand in a retaliatory fight with the Calgary Flames' Jarome Iginla, this after missing 16 games because of a concussion from the initial hit. And on it went. Defenseman Ladislav Smid had to have a bulging disc in his neck repaired, Ales Hemsky left the lineup to have reconstructive shoulder surgery. A total of seven players underwent surgery that season. There were even players stricken with the H1N1 flu.

A total of 40 players suited up for Edmonton that year. At one point there were 22 players out of the lineup, so many that only Andrew Cogliano, Dustin Penner, and Tom Gilbert played all 82 games. By the time the season came to merciful close, the Oilers had lost a staggering 531 man-games to injury. It was a franchise record, obliterating the previous mark of 346 in 2007–08.

"Some are fluke injuries. That's part of the game," Gilbert said that spring. "Some are hard to avoid. But the swine flu? Mono? I don't know what it is. We just seem to catch everything."

Dark Days

The injuries that plagued the 2009–10 Oilers were one more sore spot during a dark season. The Oilers won just one game in a 21-game midseason stretch, and players eventually tuned out Coach Pat Quinn. Souray said he'd take one for the team and waive his no-trade clause then months later demanded a trade, stating he'd been mistreated by management.

Following a New Year's Eve loss to the Flames, the Oilers and their wives and girlfriends reportedly racked up a $17,000 bill at a Calgary restaurant and then got into a dispute with the owner over payment. The story garnered national attention. More unwanted attention for a team in turmoil.

While rehabbing his back in Arizona, Khabibulin was facing speeding and impaired driving charges. Because his blood alcohol content was more than double the legal limit, the impaired charge was upgraded to an extreme DUI. (He was found guilty that summer, submitted an appeal, then later withdrew it so he could report to training camp prior to the 2011–12 season. He served the first 15 days of his sentence in Arizona's Tent City, the other 15 under house arrest.)

General manager Steve Tambellini followed through on his assertion that there would be a top-to-bottom rebuild. Assistant GM Kevin Prendergast was released after two decades with the team, as were medical trainer Ken Lowe and equipment men Barrie Stafford and Lyle Kulchisky—all long-serving, hardworking professionals who were blameless casualties. American Hockey League coach Rob Daum was dismissed, as was scout Chris McCarthy; Quinn was bumped into an advisory role, and Tom Renney was elevated to the head coaching post.

The lineup underwent changes too. Captain Ethan Moreau was placed on waivers, and the disgruntled Souray, who was asked to stay away from camp while the team continued looking for a trade partner, was eventually loaned to the Washington Capitals. The Oilers bought out Robert Nilsson's contract and didn't renew several others, opening up spots for a wave of new players, starting with Taylor Hall. Hall was selected first overall at the June draft—the first of four overall draft picks the Oilers would secure over the next six seasons. The 2010–11 Oilers finished 30th. There were 286 games lost to injury.

86 Music Box

There was once an unwritten rule in the Edmonton Oilers quarters that on game days the doors to the dressing room were to remain closed until 4:00 in the afternoon. It afforded the training staff a two-hour breather, their calm before the chaos. "Then at 4:00, that stereo came on," said Barrie Stafford, who ran the trainers' room for almost three decades. Today's Oilers have pregame playlists, victory songs, and typically a DJ who negotiates the wide variety of musical tastes.

Music has long been an integral part of dressing rooms in the NHL—iPods replaced CDs, which replaced cassette tapes; boom boxes gave way to wireless Bluetooth speakers. In the club's early days, the players even took their tape deck on the road. "The players bought a fancy stereo, a ghetto blaster, but we had a trunk built for it," said Stafford. "We carried it on trips."

Step This Way

There is an unspoken rule in the confines of most of the dressing rooms that it is sacrilege to step on the team logo that is woven into a carpet—no matter how inconveniently it may be positioned. Those who do not watch their step are subject to the indignation of players, team officials, or both.

Remember the commotion that arose when Canadian singer Justin Bieber posed for a pic with the Stanley Cup while standing on the Chicago Blackhawks logo? The Blackhawks often rope off their logo during the playoffs when space is at a premium.

The Oilers covered up their logo with a piece of carpet and/or a bin for the jerseys, so when the room was open to the media in Rexall Place, it wasn't an issue. When they moved to their new digs in downtown Edmonton, the logo was incorporated into the ceiling.

Eventually the NHL trainers decreed that every room be outfitted with a sound system as part of their standardization protocol. Ear plugs were not included. And in between renovation projects at Rexall Place, Stafford's office was located on the other side of the weight room. All that separated the two areas was a pane of glass. "That music would just be blaring. I couldn't get any work done when they were in there," he said.

He continued, "I hate rap. I hated heavy metal music, and they'd play the same music over and over and over. I'd tell them, 'Hey, I'm not going to play Andrea Bocelli when you're in there because you're going to want to pull your hair out.' So there'd be one guy in charge, and they'd find a happy medium.

"But the team typically had a theme song when we won, which was great. Whatever it was, I didn't give a crap, because it meant we had won."

87 Open Net Eludes Stefan; Play Lives in Infamy

Stuff happens. Goaltenders inexplicably surrender shots from center ice; defensemen put pucks into their own nets. And then there's Patrik Stefan. The Dallas Stars forward is the author of a blooper that continues to live in infamy. "I thought I'd seen everything, but this was one for the decades," said Stars goaltender Marty Turco.

With mere seconds left on the clock, his team up 5–4, a turnover on his stick, and an open net yawning, Stefan whiffed on his breakaway backhand then fell as he tried to recover from his mistake. Before anyone could say what the heck happened, Ales Hemsky had scored the tying goal at the other end of the rink.

Much to Stefan's relief, the Stars still managed to get out of town with two points after beating the Oilers 6–5 in a shootout.

"I'm glad I'm on a [Canadian road] trip," Stefan said after the game, which was played on January 4, 2007. "I can see it a million more times on TV."

"We were bestowed a miracle," Oilers head coach Craig MacTavish said in his postgame address at Rexall Place, duly noting that his team had surrendered a 4–1 lead. "I've never seen anything like it.... Something like that happens, and you should get a trophy. At least we turned a disaster into a debacle."

Stefan was drafted first overall by the Atlanta Thrashers in 1999, before the Vancouver Canucks selected Daniel and Henrik Sedin with the second and third selections. His last season in the league was that 2006–07 campaign, although he didn't leave the game. In 2016 he was working as an agent in the Detroit area.

"You think it's over, and then [Hemsky's] flying at the net with speed," Turco said. "I got a piece of it, but he got it in. As it was, it was a heck of a last nine seconds. The Oilers got a point, and I'm sure the fans haven't roared like that since last year's playoffs."

88 Pound for Pound

In days gone by, players would work their way into game shape during the course of a training camp, an approach that has long since been supplanted by rigorous off-season programs. But even since it has become expected that players report in extraordinary shape, there have been some rather weighty issues around the Oilers' quarters. Theo Peckham, Dustin Penner, and Georges Laraque, to name a few, were all called out for tipping the scales a little too far.

"When [Craig MacTavish] was coaching, I had to weigh in every day. I couldn't be any heavier than 255 pounds," said Laraque, who confessed he was pushing 300 pounds since he quit playing. "One day I was 256, so MacT sent me home and told me I had to get under it or I couldn't play. [I] came back and weighed 254...then I ate and ate."

When the players reported for an abbreviated camp during the lockout-shortened 2012–13 season, Peckham's weight and conditioning were so much of a concern that he spent all but four of the 48 games in the press box as a healthy scratch. The talk around town was that he was up to 265 pounds, a number he disputed, but he never denied he had to work at keeping weight off.

Penner was the target of much criticism when he scored 17 goals in a first-line role during the 2008–09 season. Head coach Craig MacTavish even chewed out the $4.25-million-a-year winger publicly at one point, stating that Penner had "never been fit enough to help" the team. Eventually dealt to the Los Angeles Kings, talk of Penner's weight didn't fade. He showed up at one camp weighing between 242 and 243 pounds, which, according to GM Dean Lombardi, was 18 pounds less than he weighed when he was traded from Edmonton.

"I tried this new thing where I close my eyes when I step on the scale and I don't find out until the media guide comes out. It's more exciting that way," Penner quipped in a conversation with Helene Elliott of the *Los Angeles Times*.

Penner, who last played for the Washington Capitals during the 2013–14 season, was also the center of much mirth while he was still with the Kings, when he suffered back spasms the morning of a game. It just so happened he was eating pancakes at the time, which he happened to mention when he was talking about the injury.

To his credit, he played along with all the mockery that followed, and even sponsored a Pancakes with Penner breakfast at a local IHOP to raise money for charity. Then he was traded from Anaheim to Washington on March 4, 2014...which also happened to be National Pancake Day.

89 Finally, a Big Fish

With playoff runs nothing more than a memory and the city of Edmonton deemed to be one of the least favorable destinations for NHL free agents, it has not been easy for the Oilers to reel in players. It hasn't been from a lack of trying.

After Daryl Katz purchased the team in 2008, he promptly opened up his pocketbook and the hockey operations department pulled out all the stops in an attempt to lure Marian Hossa to Edmonton. Hossa turned down a multiyear deal that would have paid him $9 million a season to play for the Oilers and signed a one-year $7.45 million deal with the Detroit Red Wings instead. "I know myself; I made the right decision," Hossa said of the Oilers' pitch, "but it wasn't easy to throw that much money away. I've said before, I want to have the best chance to win the Stanley Cup, and I feel like Detroit is the team." The Red Wings lost the Cup to the Pittsburgh Penguins that season, an ironic twist given that Hossa had been in a Pens jersey before he signed with Detroit. Hossa finally won his first Stanley Cup with the Chicago Blackhawks in 2010.

The Oilers, meanwhile, fell short time and again in pursuit of a big fish. Dany Heatley vetoed a trade between Edmonton and the Ottawa Senators; Michael Nylander agreed to a contract only to undergo a change of heart before putting pen to paper, and instead signed with the Washington Capitals. (The story goes that his wife was digging in her stilettos, sobbing that a move to Edmonton would put them was too far from their friends out East. This, a year after Chris Pronger's wife had had enough of the city after just one season, prompting the club's star defenseman to ask for a trade.)

And that wasn't the end of the snubs. A few summers later, winger David Clarkson turned down Edmonton's lucrative offer of $42 million spread over seven years to sign a seven-year, $36.75 million contract with the Toronto Maple Leafs. Clarkson put up just five goals and six assists in his first 60 games with the Maple Leafs, then 15 points in the next 58 games he played, before Toronto conceded the contract was an expensive mistake and flipped him to the Columbus Blue Jackets. It was a mistake the Oilers avoided only because Clarkson wanted to play in his hometown.

But in the summer of 2016, something changed. A big fish wanted to swim upstream. Milan Lucic, a tough, burly left-winger being courted by a number of teams—some offering longer terms,

It's a Small World After All

Did you know there's another link connecting Milan Lucic to the Oilers (aside from his seven-year, $42 million contract)? In 2006 the Bruins selected the native of Vancouver, British Columbia, with the 50th pick overall—a pick they had acquired from the Oilers in exchange for sending trade-deadline rental Sergei Samsonov to Edmonton.

Peter Chiarelli had been anointed GM of the Bruins weeks before that draft. Lucic didn't discount that tie either. He stated on the opening day of free agency in 2016 that aside from the appeal of playing in a glitzy state-of-the-art new arena, and playing alongside the gifted Connor McDavid, it only made sense to play for Chiarelli again. The two share memories of a 2011 Stanley Cup victory. "I had been with him for eight years in Boston, and I saw what he was able to do there. He wants to win, and that's the big thing," said Lucic.

"Finally, [the Oilers'] 2006 second-round pick has shown up—10 years later. It's almost like it was meant to be."

others more cash—chose to sign with Edmonton, affording him the chance to play with star center Connor McDavid.

"The McDavid factor changes it all," Lucic said after signing a seven-year, $42 million contract at the age of 28. "An opportunity to play with a player like that doesn't come around too often. I truly believe that in a couple of years we're going to be contending for the Stanley Cup because we have a player like that. It's about time this team starts heading in the right direction, and I just wanted to be a part of that."

90 Changing Tides

During his first postmortem as Oilers general manager, Peter Chiarelli admitted he had anticipated some "heavy lifting" when he took on the task of refitting the franchise. He had also projected an 82-point season in 2015–16, not the 70-point campaign that saw the club sink to 29th place.

More change was a certainty for Edmonton—and it began with an attention-grabbing trade that sent Taylor Hall to the New Jersey Devils for defenseman Adam Larsson. Jaws dropped, eyebrows soared. But trading an accomplished left-winger for a stay-at-home defenseman turned out to be much easier to stomach when the 2016–17 Oilers strode into the postseason.

"It was necessary to put a team together. We had a collection of great players but weren't a real good team. We were overloaded in one area and short in another," Coach Todd McLellan told Postmedia's Terry Jones before Edmonton made its first playoff appearance since 2006. "We believed we were bringing a player in of equally high quality and character as Taylor, just in a different position, and maybe not as flashy and not as recognizable. But we believed Adam Larsson was somebody who could help us compete in our division and help us defend.

"The Taylor trade was difficult for everybody to accept, but we looked at it as not only gaining Larsson but the ability to go get Milan Lucic.... We felt we got two big, strong, heavy, experienced pieces that we gave up one tremendous forward to get."

For those fans unsettled by the Hall deal that off-season—and there were plenty voicing their opinions on social media—a dose of counterirritant came with the acquisition of free agent Milan Lucic.

Chiarelli also flipped the underachieving Nail Yakupov to the St. Louis Blues for a prospect and a draft pick—an indictment of the 2012 first-round pick's play—then used the salary savings to acquire free agent defenseman Kris Russell.

With the gifted Connor McDavid up front and Cam Talbot shining in goal, the Oilers went on to finish eighth overall, thanks to their first 100-point season since 1986–87. "This team had its troubles over the years, but those days are over," said Patrick Maroon, who was added to the fold during the 2015–16 season.

"Leading up to this year, we talked about erasing the past," said Lucic. "We're kind of turning the page on everything that's happened."

The Oilers were in the hunt for the division title right up until the final game of the 2017 regular season, McLellan was shortlisted for the Coach of the Year honors that spring, and McDavid won the scoring title. The tide had indeed turned.

Hall, meanwhile, said before the playoffs began that while he was happy for the friends he left behind, he couldn't help but wrestle with a bout of jealousy. Selected first overall in 2010, he was the face of the franchise, the dynamic winger who regularly led the team in scoring, but after spending six years toiling for the club, playing for five different head coaches, he was dealt to the Devils.

He registered 20 goals and 33 assists in his first season with New Jersey, tying Kyle Palmieri for the team lead, in spite of missing several weeks because of knee surgery. The Devils did not make the playoffs. "Now that I'm seven seasons in, it's tough to watch, knowing that I haven't experienced a playoff game yet," Hall said.

"It sucks for Taylor that part of the solution for us was grabbing Larsson, but it could have happened to any of us," Jordan Eberle told Dan Barnes of the *Edmonton Journal*. The longest-serving Oiler, Eberle had played 500 games with the team before he finally stepped onto the ice for a playoff game. He had been 16 the last time the Oilers were in the playoffs, McDavid had been 9, and Talbot 19, playing for the Hamilton Red Wings in the Ontario Junior Hockey League. The first iPhone hadn't even been released. "It's been a long time for our group, our organization, and the city," McLellan said.

"I'm just really happy for the organization and I'm happy for Daryl Katz and I'm particularly happy for Oilers fans," Craig MacTavish, the club's senior vice president of hockey operations told Jones. "It's really great to have this for long-term Oilers fans who have hung in through thick and thin—and there's been a lot of thin in the last number of years.... We have this incredible new building, and it looks like the team is going to be good for a while."

91 A Hot Ticket

Owning a memento as a team enthusiast has its price. A customized jersey from the Oilers store will set you back $199.99, a ball cap in the neighborhood of $25. A jersey signed by Connor McDavid from Card Sharks memorabilia shop in West Edmonton Mall can be yours for $899.95. An autographed puck from McDavid's days with the Erie Otters? $349.95.

Take a stroll through the Oilers store in Kingsway Mall to check their official team wares, or mosey over to Pro Am Sports in St. Albert, where there's an abundance of collectibles to choose from. An unsigned 11x14 photo of Connor McDavid's first goal celebration? $17.95. An Oilers puck signed by Jordan Eberle? $89.95.

But an Edmonton family took it a step further during the team's move from Rexall Place to Rogers Place. The family members, who co-own MGS, a local company that supplies granite and quartz countertops, paid $14,275 US for a 10-foot Oilers sign in an online auction. Bidding started at $500. "First of all, it's for charity, something that we like. [Second,] all three families love the Oilers," Angela He told CBC.ca. "It's iconic and historic, and we want it to stay in Edmonton."

A long list of pieces from the Oilers' first home were auctioned off after the 2015–16 season—including the massive sign that hung on the northeast exterior of the arena. The six-foot-wide carpeted logo that sat on the dressing room floor sold for $3,505 US to physician Travis Webster of Bonnyville. He was planning to use the carpet in his man cave in his new home. The monies raised from the auction went to the Edmonton Community Foundation.

Angela He, along with her siblings, also paid $6,335 for a 600-pound metal 25th anniversary sign that once hung in the arena concourse. It is now hanging in their office. The Oilers sign is hanging on the exterior of their south side building. Underneath they added the message: DIE HARD FANS OF THE EDMONTON OILERS.

"It's exactly what we are, and it's exactly the reason that we bought it," Angela He said. "We don't miss any games. We don't miss anything with the Oilers."

"We're whole-time Oilers fans, not just longtime," Angela He added of their two purchases. "We did the right thing. We will always be a part it."

92 Frozen in Time

If you're looking for an iconic landmark, you need not look any further than the larger-than-life bronze statue of Wayne Gretzky holding the Stanley Cup high over his head. For 27 years, the 9'2" effigy stood on the north side of the Oilers' first home. It greeted game-goers, served as a reliable meeting place, and was regularly featured in fans' pictures—right up until the day it was moved to the new arena.

Funded by Molson Brewery and gifted to the City of Edmonton, the 950-pound statue was the creation of sculptor John Weaver in conjunction with Don Begg at Begg's Studio West Bronze Foundry & Art Gallery in Cochrane, Alberta. It was unveiled on August 27, 1989, during a civic tribute during a ceremony at the Northlands Coliseum. "To me the statue symbolizes what was most important to everyone…that was winning," Gretzky said that summer day. "To have me standing with my gloves and stick didn't seem fitting. Holding the Stanley Cup…that kind of summed everything up here…. I hope when people walk past it, they think of the good

A fan poses with the statue before Game 4 of the 2006 Stanley Cup Finals.

times I tried to give them. I hope they think, *It was fun to watch him play.*"

The star returned to Edmonton for the event, consequently drawing 14,000 devoted fans back to the arena for the occasion. It mattered not that just a few short months earlier, Gretzky and the Los Angeles Kings had defeated the Oilers in the Smythe Division semifinals. Accompanied by his parents, as well as his wife, Janet, and their baby daughter, Paulina, Gretzky also received a key to the city from Mayor Terry Cavanagh, who was among those on hand to thank the Great One for 10 memorable seasons.

Noticeably absent from the festivities were owner Peter Pocklington, who had sold Gretzky to Los Angeles one year earlier, and general manager Glen Sather. The official word from the club was that it was against team policy to honor a player before he'd retired. Because the statue belonged to the city, there was also some debate as to whether or not it would move with the team to the new arena. Prudence prevailed.

"When I think back to that time, I think, *Good God, we won four Stanley Cups in five years,* and then I think about the skinny kid who led the charge," former team president Patrick LaForge was quoted as saying during the debate. "His statue captures the greatest memories of people at a time when I think everyone in Edmonton stood an inch or two taller."

The statue is now standing on 104th Avenue, near the southwest entrance to Rogers Place. Before it was moved, it was loaded by crane into the back of a pickup truck and returned to the Cochrane studio for cleaning and refurbishing. "I would like to have a penny for every photograph that's been taken," Begg said when he returned to Edmonton to pick up the statue. Weaver passed away, at the age of 92, in 2012. "That's what it was made to do," Begg continued, "to honor the Oilers and Wayne and to show that this was somebody of great importance, and it has done that. I'm glad we were a part of it."

Paving the Way

So how do a city and its hockey team honor one of the game's greatest players when he leaves the game? Aside from a splashy, sold-out pregame banner-raising ceremony—the first to be staged in Edmonton? With a stretch of paved road. The freeway that runs alongside the arena—often affectionately known as the House That Wayne Built—was renamed Wayne Gretzky Drive on October 1, 1999, the day his jersey was retired. That night, with the New York Rangers in Edmonton for the Oilers season opener, Gretzky made one final lap around the arena, in the back of a black pickup truck. Highlights of his extraordinary career flashed on the scoreboard. Voices cracked, tears flowed as a legend said good-bye.

"I have nothing but great thoughts and great memories," Gretzky told the *Edmonton Journal*'s Dan Barnes that fall. "It was a wonderful 21 years. Unfortunately for all of us, something happens. We get old. I understood that as much as anyone. People often say to me, 'My goodness, you're doing well.' I am. I'm content. I'm at peace of mind. Do I miss it? Absolutely I miss it. I wish I was at training camp right now. I wish I was playing. I'd be lying if I said I wasn't but I just couldn't play as good as I used to, in my mind. That's why it was time to move along.... One of the great things about retiring is you get people who come up to you and say 'I wish you would have played one more year.' As an athlete that's all you can ask for. You can't have a nicer thing said to you."

His No. 99 was also retired by the National Hockey League.

As for Gretzky's decision to wear the No. 99, that stems back to the 1977–78 season he spent with the Sault Ste. Marie Greyhounds of the Ontario Hockey Association. Gretzky had wanted to wear the No. 9, to pay homage to his idol, Gordie Howe, but the number was being worn by veteran Soo teammate Brian Gualazzi. It was Greyhounds coach Murray "Muzz" MacPherson who suggested Gretzky wear No. 99. And for 20 sublime years in the NHL, that was the only number he wore.

"He came to us as a kid, became a man, and then a legend," Oilers general manager Glen Sather said during the ceremony. "We'll always think of Wayne as ours. Playing for the Oilers was a perfect fit."

93 Giving Back

Tucked into the neighborhood of McCauley, in Edmonton's inner city, sits an outdoor rink covered with the fingerprints of former Oilers. From the time it is cold enough to make ice until it is too warm to keep the rink open, the facility is a haven for local youth, some of whom desperately need an outlet.

The McCauley rink project was spearheaded by former Oilers captain Al Hamilton, at the urging of former head coach Ted Green. Hamilton joined forces with Father Jim Holland, from nearby Sacred Heart Church, and the result is a facility that provides all the necessities. A donated retrofitted camp trailer serves as the dressing room, another local company stepped up and resurfaced the rink surface, and on it went. Full-time staff now manage the facility; there are donated sticks and skates, helmets and gloves available for the kids who drop by—upward of 30 per night. There's even advertising on the rink boards.

"They didn't have anything there. They had a set of old boards," said Hamilton, "and a trailer that two or three guys were sleeping under. Everything was run-down. Over the past seven years, we've received donations and raised money, and now we even have a management team on-site that runs the rink in the winter months.... There's a lot of satisfaction from that project. I always have a smile on my face when I'm there."

In 1990 an outdoor rink opened in the neighborhood, but the McCauley Community League didn't have the money to maintain it. Sometimes it was a challenge just to get the ice in. Now there's even a storage area for the donated equipment. Former Oilers equipment manager Lyle Kulchisky was even recruited by

Hamilton to manage the project after the Oilers cut ties with their long-serving training staff.

"He sets the rules. He's grouchy, but the kids love him," said Hamilton. "He'll usually have a pot of chili or something cooking out there, so they have something to eat. It certainly turned out to be a bigger project than I thought it would, but it's rewarding.... It's a place for those kids to go. There's no organized games. We just want them to go out and play shinny or go skating, and everything is there for them. They can just go out and have fun.... It's a welcome break for some of them."

In 2015 the project received a check for $60,000 from Hockey Canada and the Edmonton Oilers Community Foundation to add players' boxes, a penalty box, netting, and other add-ons that were lacking.

There's an annual Family Day skating party that has drawn upward of 300 people; Norwood School has brought students out, some of whom have never been on ice before, and once a year, beat officers from the Downtown Division are at the rink to contest the McCauley Cup in a game of shinny hockey. "Every year [the officers] look forward to it. It's a good break for them, to get off the streets

In Memory

The Jamie Platz Family YMCA, located in Edmonton's West End, was named after a young Oilers fan who was diagnosed with a spinal tumor when he was just 18 months old. By the time he was 10, Platz had undergone 68 operations—a story that was shared in 1985 when he required an expensive procedure that could only be performed in Mexico. The ensuing media campaign not only raised donations, it caught the attention of owner Peter Pocklington.

In spite of the treatments and another four operations, the tumors spread, and in 1987, at the age of 12, young Jamie Platz lost his fight with the detestable disease. When fund-raising began to build the YMCA, Pocklington's donation of $1 million meant he was entitled to name the building. He chose Jamie Platz.

and to be dealing with the community members in a different light," Constable Terrance Jakubowski said during the 2015 contest. "Any positive interaction we can have, to take the negativity away from the perception of policing, is beneficial to us. These small interactions with the kids at a younger age benefit our future as a society. If they can see a police officer playing side by side in just a friendly game, hopefully they will see the police in a different light," Jakubowski continued. "The support we have gotten for this event has grown over the years. It's just incredible."

94 Casting Call

Long before Richard Dean Anderson embodied the role of MacGyver in the original hit television series of the same name, his sights were set on a career as a professional hockey player. It was a dream that evaporated when he broke both his arms in separate incidents while playing for his high school team in Minnesota. As a youngster, Canadian crooner Michael Bublé was hell-bent on playing for the Vancouver Canucks—right up to the point where he realized he didn't have the requisite skills. Actor Steve Carell was also on the ice at a young age, eventually playing goal at Denison University, a Division III school in Ohio, just so he could keep himself in the game while he pursued his history degree.

But what about those professional hockey players who fancied some air time on the big screen, or even the television screen? An unabashed fan of daytime soap operas, Wayne Gretzky once secured a guest appearance on *The Young and the Restless*. Cast as a member of the Mafia, he had one line in that 1981 episode: "I'm Wayne, from the Edmonton operation." He was a guest on

Letterman in 1986, *The Tonight Show with Jay Leno,* and in 1989 he hosted *Saturday Night Live.*

Conan O'Brien had just started as a writer for the show and even had a cameo appearance in a skit called "Waikiki Hockey." Gretzky played Chad—Chad Gretzky—and not only turned out to be the hero for the Coconut Kings hockey team, he saved the night at a hotel party when he stepped up to the microphone to sing a ditty that included this cheesy line: "I slipped the puck across the goal line / the crowd went crazy and roared / But when my baby kissed me and held me in my arms / I knew that I had finally scored." The two were reunited on late night television on January 24, 2014, when Gretzky made a guest appearance on Conan's late-night talk show.

"I remember it like it was yesterday," Gretzky said of his *SNL* appearance. Turns out he found out about his role while reading a newspaper article on a flight to the Kentucky Derby with his wife, Janet Jones. She had called *SNL* producer Lorne Michaels to tell him Wayne would accept their invite to do the show.

But Gretzky wasn't the only one to test the film and television waters. Other players with Edmonton ties have had their moments. Marty McSorley, who sandwiched eight seasons with the Kings in between stints with the Oilers, played Mack the copilot in *Con Air,* a Detroit fan in *Forget Paris,* and a henchman in *Bad Boys.*

Another of the Oilers who made it to the big screen was Steve Carlson, who played 73 games with Edmonton's WHA entry after playing Steve Hanson in the original *Slap Shot* movie (he was the Hanson brother who body-checked the pop machine to get his quarter back).

The three Carlson brothers—Steve, Jack, and Jeff—were not only the inspiration for the indelible Hanson brothers, all three Minnesotans were offered roles in the 1977 film. But Jack was being recruited by the Oilers for their playoff run at the time and opted to join Edmonton rather than try his hand at acting. Instead, Dave Hanson got the part of Jack Hanson in *Slap Shot* and *Slap Shot 2.*

"Reviewers [Gene] Siskel and [Roger] Ebert gave it two thumbs down. But later they were asked by Johnny Carson whether they ever made a mistake rating a movie that had [become] a huge hit, and they said *Slap Shot*," Steve Carlson told the *Montreal Gazette's* Dave Stubbs in 2015, shortly after he turned 60.

He roomed with Wayne Gretzky in the Hall of Famer's rookie season and played with Gordie Howe before playing 52 games for the Los Angeles Kings in 1979–80—his only stint in the NHL.

The "Hanson brothers" still make yearly appearances in rinks around North America. Jack Carlson, meanwhile, finished the season with the Oilers only to be dealt to the New England Whalers in the off-season before joining the Minnesota North Stars for the first of 236 games he'd play in the NHL.

And of course this entry wouldn't be complete without a mention of Oilers owner Daryl Katz, who announced in 2015 that he was joining forces with movie producer Joel Silver to create Silver Pictures Entertainment.

95 They Said It

All too often the clichés roll off the tongues of players and coaches with a ridiculous amount of ease. Surely, you know them well:

"We need to simplify our game."

"At the end of the day…"

"We didn't play a full 60 minutes."

"It is what it is."

"We have to take it one game at a time."

"Like I said…"

And on and on and on.

But every so often there are a few gems that are actually worth repeating—such as these comments from Oilers past and present:

"What are they going to want up there next, a bucket of chicken?" —General manager Glen Sather when he spotted a bottle of water on top of the Philadelphia Flyers' net during the 1985 Stanley Cup Finals

"I said to the players today that Carolina is a little bit like carbon monoxide poisoning; you don't really sense it, you don't really sense the fear, but it's lethal." —Head Coach Craig MacTavish during the 2006 Stanley Cup Finals

"I remember thinking, *If I never play in the NHL again, at least I scored a goal.*" —Wayne Gretzky on scoring his first of 894 goals

"We sucked the hind banana." —Coach Pat Quinn after a 6–0 loss to the Colorado Avalanche in 2009–10

"Because there wasn't time to play 54." —Goaltender Grant Fuhr when asked how he could play 36 holes of golf in the middle of the Stanley Cup playoffs

"Stressful? Do you know a lot of jobs where every time you make a mistake, a red light goes off over your head and 15,000 people start booing?" —Goaltender Jacques Plante, whose Hall of Fame career ended with the WHA Oilers

"I was just trying to get on a Top 10 list for something. And I'm pretty sure that might make it for this week." —Backup goaltender Richard Bachman after Drew Doughty's shot from center ice ended up in the back of the Oilers' net (the Oilers went on to defeat the Los Angeles Kings 4–2)

"You've got to have a long stick to score from the bench." —Petr Klima on his lack of ice time during the 1990 playoffs

"When I got married, I half expected to see him at the altar in a tux." —Gretzky on his on-ice shadow, Steve Kasper

"I know some of them have skill, I watch them in the morning, but some guys are really morning glories." —Coach Pat Quinn

"Wayne was like the Pope. This was like taking the Pope from Italy to Canada." —Los Angeles Kings owner Bruce McNall on acquiring Gretzky from the Oilers

"Edmonton has offered a mostly inflated salary for a player, and I think it's an act of desperation for a general manager who is fighting to keep his job." —Anaheim GM Brian Burke after his Edmonton counterpart, Kevin Lowe, signed Dustin Penner to a five-year, $21.25 million US offer sheet

"He reminds me of the Wizard of Oz. You comb his hair, put a white shirt on, wheel him out in front of the camera, and he'll say whatever you guys want." —Craig MacTavish, in the midst of the feud between Lowe and Burke

"They play a little bit like a junior team, I think, sometimes. They take a lot of risks, a lot of chances. They're a little all over the place. There's not a lot of structure always in their game." —Montreal Canadiens forward Lars Eller before taking on the 2–6–1 Oilers

"They might as well have sent me over a fruit basket and a bottle of wine." —Oilers coach Dallas Eakins on using Eller's comments for motivation in a 4–3 win

"I've told my wife she can only shop at Mac's. I don't know how long we're staying here." —Bill Huard, on being linked to trade talks with the Pittsburgh Penguins

"I actually sleep better after a loss than I do a win...I have been sleeping a lot." —Oilers coach Tom Renney

kreatuorelyly

"How would you like that guy operating on you with those hands?" — Don Cherry on defenseman Randy Gregg, a doctor, missing a wide-open net

"Jason Arnott will be here as long as I'm here, for the time being." —Glen Sather on the Arnott trade rumors that were circulating in 1997

"You miss 100 percent of the shots you never take." —Wayne Gretzky

"I just tape four Tylenols to it." —Boris Mironov on dealing with a sore ankle

"Tell him he's Wayne Gretzky." —Coach Ted Green when he heard Shaun Van Allen didn't know where he was or who he was after he'd been concussed

"There should be a league rule that he has to be passed around from team to team every year." —Boston Bruins coach Terry O'Reilly on Wayne Gretzky

"The only way you can check Gretzky is to hit him when he is standing still singing the national anthem." —Boston Bruins general manager Harry Sinden

"I remember my first year. I hit him with three good punches and couldn't believe he was still standing. He hit me with one and cracked my helmet. My head hurt for a week." —Enforcer Georges Laraque speaking about peer Stu Grimson

"I won't miss him. Maybe the West Edmonton Mall will miss him, but not me." —Glen Sather after leaving Andrei Kovalenko exposed in the expansion draft

96 Desert Drought

In one of those hard-to-figure anomalies, the Arizona Coyotes had an unshakable dominance over the Oilers that transcended five head coaches, numerous roster shuffles, and one managerial shakeup. Game after game, season after season, the Coyotes registered at least a point against Edmonton.

The curse of the Coyotes started on January 25, 2011—the last time Edmonton beat the Desert Dogs for almost six years—and lasted until December 21, 2016, when the Oilers registered a 3–2 win in Arizona. In short, the Coyotes played 25 games over a span of nearly six years without a loss in regulation (21–0–4).

"Every year is a new group, but we've won now," said Todd McLellan, the fifth of the coaches to experience the phenomenon with the Oilers. "That team has cleaned our clock. We just found a way to come out on the winning end."

When McLellan was with the San Jose Sharks, it was the Buffalo Sabres causing the vexation—although nothing as unfathomable as the Coyotes' reign over the Oilers. "It didn't matter what we did or who we put on the ice or where we played, we had trouble with [the Sabres]," said McLellan. "That's just the way it was…. I'm aware of the past year and a half [of] history [here in Edmonton], but it obviously goes deeper than that."

In the first of the games the teams played in 2016–17, Edmonton went into the game holding down the first spot in the Pacific Division with a record of 12–8–1. The Coyotes were 29th in the league (6–10–2), but in the end, nothing changed. Arizona won 3–2 in a shootout, stretching their dominance to 24 games

(20–0–4), and then just two nights later, the teams met again in Edmonton and the Coyotes scored a 2–1 win.

The last time a team had shown that kind of dominance over an opponent was when the Philadelphia Flyers went 32 games without a regulation loss to the Los Angeles Kings from October 22, 1974, until February 5, 1983. The NHL record was set by the Montreal Canadiens in their first 34 games against Washington.

Now it would be easy to just point to the Oilers' struggles against every team in the league, given that the team took up permanent residence in the lower half of the standings for so many years, but the Coyotes have had their dog days too…unless they were playing Edmonton. In 2014–15 both teams won just 24 games. Five of Arizona's wins were against Edmonton. The Coyotes finished 29th overall that spring, the Oilers 28th based on their overtime points, but they still managed to win the lottery and the rights to phenom Connor McDavid.

"I don't have any reasons why they have had our number," said Jordan Eberle, "but when I came into the league it was Minnesota we couldn't beat." Ah yes, Minnesota. Between 2007 and 2016, the Wild were 21–3–1 in games against Edmonton in St. Paul. Overall, they had 47 wins, the majority of which came after the 2004–05 lockout. When they began to play in Minnesota in 2000, and for the next three years, the Oilers were 13–2–4–2.

97 #timeshavechanged

Can't get to the game? No prob. With today's online platforms, there's no shortage of ways to keep tabs on the happenings on the ice. And off. At last count, the Edmonton Oilers had a staff of 14 providing content for numerous social media feeds linked to both Rogers Place and the team. There are in-game updates available on the team's Twitter feed, as well as countless other accounts from other outlets. The postgame interviews are uploaded to the Oilers' website; the pregame preamble is there too. A live stream of the postgame can be viewed on Facebook—photos, highlights…it's all available ICYMI.

Social media is now as much a part of the hockey routine as morning skates and practice sessions. In 2015 Alex Ovechkin had a league-high 1.52 million followers on Twitter. By 2016 that number had climbed to 2.53 million, and that was for just 630 tweets.

Players have their own feeds, as do the teams. Fans have their forums. This new cyber world has required the Oilers to regularly expand their online team. There are writers and video producers, content managers and web developers, on-air reporters and game-day hosts. In 2015–16 Edmonton ranked second behind the Montreal Canadiens in web traffic in almost every major metric. And that was a season in which the team finished 29th.

"I wouldn't enjoy it," said Al Hamilton, who left the NHL's Buffalo Sabres in 1972 to play for the Oilers in the WHA. "Your life is public enough, and if you let yourself get into all that stuff, somewhere along the way you're opening yourself up to a hell of a lot of unnecessary criticism."

Dallas Eakins, during his time as the Oilers' head coach, would go so far as to tweet lineup changes and his starting goaltender. "I think it's my duty, especially when we're on the road, to let our fans know what's going on," he said of his Twitter usage. "The second part for me is inspiration. I get lots of inspiration off of Twitter. People's stories, things like that. I think it's our job [as coaches] to try to inspire as well. The problem with Twitter is when you talk to the players about it, it's an easy place for people to type and snipe. It has turned into a very negative place. That's where I'm not sure what the feedback is. I learned a few years ago, when I was with the [Toronto] Marlies, don't go read what they're saying about your name on Twitter, because it's not going to be good."

Days after signing on to Twitter as Nail10_1993 during the Oilers' rookie camp, Nail Yakupov picked up 19,983 followers. Connor McDavid had 195,000 followers after 65 games in the NHL—and he'd posted just four tweets between September 4 and November 10. One was a retweet. The Oilers' team account has gathered 616,000 followers in McDavid's sophomore season—give or take a few thousand.

"Social media has become such a big part of society and professional sports, and yeah, we do need to manage it to a point, but we certainly don't try to control them," J. J. Hebert, the Oilers' director of media relations said when the landscape really started to shift. "We encourage our guys to have character and to interact with the fans."

The NHL issued a league directive in 2011 stipulating that there was to be a blackout period on game days. Players are not to engage on social media two hours before the opening faceoff and not until they have finished their postgame media obligations. The league and the NHL Players' Association established the social media policy, following the lead of the NFL and the NBA. During the 2016–17 season, the league was live-streaming games on Twitter.

"Now you're inundated with information—sometimes good stuff, but more often I think it's an avenue for people just to voice their opinion," said Hamilton. "I didn't need somebody to tell me I played crappy. I know if I did."

98 A Seasoned View of It All

The first hockey game Rod Phillips ever called for a radio broadcast was a nerve-rattling, voice-cracking blur. He was working for CFRN radio in 1973, cohosting the late-night weekend sportscast when he was assigned the play-by-play gig for a World Hockey Association game between the Oilers and the Winnipeg Jets. The station had secured the rights to the games and wanted to lock down a broadcaster.

"The first game I ever did for the Oilers was the first time I had ever broadcast a hockey game," said Phillips. "I was never so scared in my life...but it worked out. Five minutes into the game, I thought, *Oh, man, this is too good to be true.*" He honed his craft, listening to other broadcasters, in particular his icon Danny Gallivan, and as he put it, he "got to be not bad at it."

He was better than not bad. He was the Voice of the Oilers, the passionate orator from Calmar, Alberta, who called 3,542 games before calling it a career. In 2003 Phillips received the Foster Hewitt Memorial Award during the Hockey Hall of Fame inductions.

"I feel fortunate. I think some guys retire then regret it. I never did," said Phillips, who announced his retirement in 2010, then called 10 games in the 2010–11 season. "I was absolutely blessed to have this job. Not a lot of guys get the opportunity I did."

The Other Route to the Media Wing of the Hall of Fame

Jim Matheson tagged along with his father, Jack, from one sporting event to another so often that one would have presumed his path had been paved long before he started chronicling the fortunes and failures of the Oilers.

But the younger Matheson initially had no intention of following in the footsteps of his father, the decorated sports journalist who carved out his illustrious career in Winnipeg. "I got used to my dad taking me to things, and I felt very privileged…but I was going to university [to study history and political science]," he said.

Jim Matheson was in his first year of studies when the University of Winnipeg offered to cover his $500 tuition if he covered their sports teams. But he didn't really appreciate the business until he went to Regina to work at the *Leader-Post*, and there was no looking back after that.

When the Oilers were playing in the WHA, Matheson was on the beat. He was at the airport when Wayne Gretzky, then 17, was ferried into Edmonton on Nelson Skalbania's private jet, and he was in the press box for each of the five Stanley Cups—as well as the decade-long playoff drought. He even worked on the radio broadcast with Rod Phillips when the games were carried on CFRN. Together they witnessed the sky highs and the rock bottoms of the franchise.

"They were so good to me my first year, showing me around, telling me who to talk to," said Morley Scott, who joined Phillips in the booth in 1993. "We were in Montreal, early in my first year, and my job then was to interview the opposing coach. I was looking for Jacques Demers, and I couldn't find him anywhere. The dressing room was almost empty too, and then a trainer said to me, 'He's done for the day. He's not doing any more media.' All I'm thinking is, *Crap, I'm in trouble.*"

Scott, still not sure what he was going to do, had just finished communicating his dilemma when Matheson got out of his seat, told the color man to follow him, and set off under the stands, through the Canadiens' dressing room, and into the labyrinth that was the hallway in the bowels of the Forum. "Matty knocks on a door, we hear 'Come in,' and it's Jacques Demers sitting in his office. Matty just says, 'This guy needs to talk to you for the pregame show,' and Jacques says, 'Okay.'"

Matheson had tucked away his Bachelor of Arts degree long ago to carve out a career that started with a paycheck of $75 a week and eventually earned him entrance into the Hockey Hall of Fame as a recipient of the Elmer Ferguson Memorial Award in 2000.

Jack Matheson passed away on January 24, 2011; Jim was back in the press box when the Oilers opened the 2016–17 season in their new arena.

99 Chasing the Calder

More than a smattering of Oilers have had their names inscribed on the trophies awarded annually to those players who have had standout seasons in the NHL—with one notable exception: the Calder Memorial Trophy. Even though five of the team's draft picks carved out careers that led to an induction into the Hall of Fame, even though the team selected first overall in four drafts, an Oiler has not captured Rookie of the Year honors. Not the Great One...not even the Next One.

Connor McDavid was the fourth Oiler to have made the final ballot, following Ryan Nugent-Hopkins (second in 2012), Jason Arnott (second in 1994), and Grant Fuhr (third in 1982). McDavid finished behind Philadelphia Flyers defenseman Shayne Gostisbehere and 2016 winner Artemi Panarin of the Chicago Blackhawks, then Auston Matthews of the Toronto Maple Leafs in 2017.

It was 36 years earlier when Wayne Gretzky netted 137 points in his first season in the NHL, which left him sharing the scoring lead with Marcel Dionne of the Los Angeles Kings, but Gretzky was deemed ineligible because he had played in the World Hockey Association. Defenseman Ray Bourque of the Boston Bruins won the Calder that year.

McDavid met the NHL's ambiguous criteria, going straight from the draft, where he was selected first overall, to the Oilers' starting lineup. Trouble was, he missed half the season with a broken collarbone. He still finished with 48 points in 45 games—on a team that finished a dismal 29th in the standings—but it wasn't enough. Panarin, 24, netted 30 goals and 47 assists for the

And the Winner Was...

Hart Memorial Trophy (Most Valuable Player)
Wayne Gretzky: 1980 straight through to 1987
Mark Messier: 1990
Connor McDavid: 2017

Vezina Trophy (Top Goaltender)
Grant Fuhr: 1988

Art Ross Trophy (Leading Scorer)
Wayne Gretzky: 1981 to 1987
Connor McDavid: 2017

James Norris Memorial Trophy (Outstanding Defenseman)
Paul Coffey: 1985 and 1986

Lady Byng Memorial Trophy (Typically Goes to the Player with Plenty of Points and the Fewest Penalty Minutes)
Wayne Gretzky: 1980
Jari Kurri: 1985

Jack Adams Trophy (Coach of the Year)
Glen Sather: 1986

Conn Smythe Trophy (Stanley Cup MVP)
Mark Messier: 1984
Wayne Gretzky: 1985 and 1988
Bill Ranford: 1990

Ted Lindsay Award (MVP as Chosen by the Players)
Wayne Gretzky: 1982 to 1985, and again in 1987
Mark Messier: 1990
Connor McDavid: 2017

King Clancy Memorial Trophy (Player Who Exemplified Leadership Qualities and Made Noteworthy Contributions to the Community)
Kevin Lowe: 1990
Ethan Moreau: 2009
Andrew Ference: 2014

Blackhawks. He had played six full seasons in the Kontinental Hockey League before signing with Chicago.

"Sure, he played pro hockey, but it's nothing like the NHL," McDavid told Postmedia. "The KHL is probably as close to the NHL as you can get, and that's obviously a benefit, but it is still his first year in the NHL, and what he did was amazing. I think he's very worthy."

As for his reflections on his first season, McDavid had this to say: "Don't go into the boards too hard; I think that's something I learned."

100 Home Sweet (New) Home

Their old home had had its day. Once the standard for new arenas—and certainly the stage on which Wayne Gretzky carved out his Hall of Fame career—Rexall Place had aged considerably. It was time to close the door, which also meant leaving behind the ghosts of seasons past. "We live in a different era now. A lot of people understood and remembered Maple Leaf Gardens, the Montreal Forum, and Chicago Stadium, and you hate to see those buildings go," said Gretzky, who attended the official ribbon cutting for Rogers Place. "Northlands Coliseum was a pretty special place, but it's a new time and a new era, and you have to change with the times. This [new] arena is truly fascinating in every aspect.… I hope they can build their own identity, this group, with this arena, and build some history here."

The 18,641-seat venue, built at a cost of almost $614 million— a cost shared by taxpayers, ticket buyers, and the Oilers—sits in the city's downtown core, and it is a showpiece. Designed to resemble a stylized oil drop, there are open concourses, massive murals behind the arena, wide seats inside, and a 46-foot-wide, 36-foot-high high-definition scoreboard.

Touted as one of the most technologically equipped venues in North America, Rogers Place opened on September 8, 2016, but it wasn't an easy road. There were years of debates and discord. Team owner Daryl Katz even made an exploratory trip to Seattle when negotiations with the city reached an impasse. When the drugstore magnate bought the team in 2008, he was adamant the city needed a downtown arena. Five years later, he finally had a deal with the city. "I couldn't believe what we'd built or what it would mean for our city," he said. "It wasn't always easy, but I think we can agree the result has been outstanding.... It really serves as a model of how public/private partnerships can be constructed for the benefit of everybody. The amount of work that went into this, the resources, the people, the time…it was an enormous undertaking, [and] to see it all come together like this is exhilarating."

It was not just an expensive undertaking; there is also a price to be paid for holding a season ticket. A pass to the upper reaches of the upper bowl was $2,600 in the rink's first year, while the view from a drink rail located on a private concourse set purchasers back a steep $15,750. It didn't matter. The 15,000 season tickets available for the first season were sold months before the rink opened. In spite of all the non-playoff seasons, there's been a waiting list for season tickets in Edmonton, dating all the way back to 2007. And now there's the glitzy new rink to draw in fans. And Connor McDavid.

Connor McDavid, who led the Oilers into the new rink as the NHL's youngest captain, is as much of a draw as the rink itself. He's also the future. The Next One. Just as Rexall was the House That Wayne Gretzky Built, Rogers now belongs to McDavid and the next wave of Oilers.

"The ice isn't quite as fast as [at] Rexall," Gretzky said, who went out for a spin in the new arena on opening day. "I seemed to be faster in the '90s than I am today. [But] this place is special, and I hope you guys make some new memories and win some more championships because the city deserves it. What makes an arena really special is when you start winning and when you win championships. They have the foundation, a good organization, some good, young players, and I wish them all the best."

"This will feel like a fresh start," said Oilers center Mark Letestu, "we can leave the past few years in the rearview."

Acknowledgments and Sources

A project like this wouldn't be possible without a multitude of sources, not the least of which were all those who set aside time to be interviewed. And of course Ryan Smyth, who also wrote the foreword. Many thanks.

Interviewees
Sam Abouhassan
Darrell Davis
Daryl Evans
Trent Evans
Chris Hamelin
Al Hamilton
Barry Hunka
Peter Jagla
Lyle Kulchisky
Patrick LaForge
Dennis Laliberte
Ken Lowe
Steve Makris
Todd Marchant
Jim Matheson
Todd McFarlane
Jill Metz
Stephen Moss
Kurtis Mucha
Jouni Nieminen
Rod Phillips
Fernando Pisani
Morley Scott

Ryan Smyth
Barrie Stafford
Rob Suggitt

Websites
CBC.ca
edmontonoilers.com
ESPN.com
greatesthockeylegends.com
HHOF.com
hockeydb.com
hockeyfights.com
NHL.com
smithsonianmag.com
Sportsnet.ca
TSN.ca
Yahoo.com

Newspapers, Magazines, and News Agencies
630 CHED
Associated Press
Canadian Press
Edmonton Journal
Edmonton Sun
Globe and Mail
Hockey News
Los Angeles Times
National Post
Postmedia
Sports Illustrated
USA Today

Books

Horton, Marc. *Voice of a City: The Edmonton Journal's First Century, 1903–2003.* Edmonton, Alberta, Canada: Edmonton Journal Group, 2004.

Hunter, Bill with Bob Weber. *Wild Bill: Bill Hunter's Legendary 65 Years in Canadian Sport.* Calgary, Alberta, Canada: Johnson Gorman Publishers, 2000.

Jones, Terry. *Edmonton's Hockey Knights, 79 to 99.* Edmonton, Alberta, Canada: Edmonton Sun, 1998.

Semenko, Dave and Larry Tucker. *Looking Out for Number One.* Lancaster, UK: Gazelle Book Services Ltd., 1989.

Turchansky, Ray. *Edmonton Oilers Hockey Club: Celebrating 25 Years in the Heartland of Hockey.* Edmonton, Alberta, Canada: Edmonton Journal Group, Inc., 2003.

Weekes, Don. *Hockey Hall of Fame Book of Trivia.* Richmond Hill, Ontario, Canada: Firefly Books, 2014.

Zeman, Gary W. *Alberta On Ice.* CITY: GMS Ventures, 1985.